The Complete Guide to Zoning

The Complete Guide to Zoning

How Real Estate Owners and
Developers Can Create and Preserve
Property Value

Dwight H. Merriam

McGraw-Hill

New York Chicago San Francisco Lisbon London
Madrid Mexico City Milan New Delhi San Juan
Seoul Singapore Sydney Toronto

4 5 6 7 8 9 0   FGR/FGR   0 9 8 7

ISBN 0-07-144379-7

McGraw-Hill books are available at special quantity discounts to use as premiums and sales promotions, or for use in corporate training programs. For more information, please write to the Director of Special Sales, Professional Publishing, McGraw-Hill, Two Penn Plaza, New York, NY 10121-2298. Or contact your local bookstore.

For Susan, Alexander, and Lucy for their support and understanding, and for helping me find the time to write.

Contents

Contents

Acknowledgments

I acknowledge the contributions of my mentors—Ted Bacon, Ed Kaiser, Dave Brower, Phil Green, Dave Godschalk, the late Jack Parker, the late Jim Webb, Quintin Johnstone, Bob Freilich, Dan Mandelker, and the late Marlin Smith—and the many peers from whom I have learned so much. Without the support of the incomparable Land-Use Group at Robinson & Cole, we could not have achieved such great success in our practice, and without the generosity of my partners in giving me the freedom to write, lecture, and teach while I practice law, I would not have been able to write this book.

Although what you read here is entirely my responsibility, I owe special thanks to great proofreaders and copyeditors. My wife, Susan; my assistant, Sue Golemon; and fellow lawyers at Robinson & Cole, Eric Lukingbeal and Frank Coulom all helped. Charles Janson, a lawyer in our Stamford office and the best copyeditor I know, spent days reworking the text. Finally, Melissa Scuereb and Janice Race at McGraw-Hill worked their magic, along with Alice Manning. Thank you all.

Introduction

Why should you read this book? Why did I write it?

You will learn enough about zoning law from reading my book—cover to cover or in bits and pieces—to get the most out of your real estate. This is true whether you own a small retirement condominium or a $100 million manufacturing facility. You will have the benefit of my more than 25 years' experience in getting big and small projects approved and built. This book gives you the basic knowledge that you need to get the job done, whether it's adding a carport to your home or rebuilding a shopping center.

Most people don't know this, but with a little strategizing and some luck, you can double or triple your property's value in one night. That's what people often hire me for—to get the local officials to change the zoning to allow more development—but you don't have to be a lawyer or a planner to do it. Zoning changes create value. It's about as easy as printing money, if you know how to do it, and it's legal.

Even professional planners and lawyers will learn some useful things from this book. Most planners (I am a certified planner as well as a lawyer) have a great interest in land-use law, but often find themselves shortchanged by the arcane legal texts available. I'm reminded of the book report by the third grader that began: "This book taught me more about penguins than I wanted to know." Law texts tell us more than we need to know in order to solve most real-world problems.

At the same time, many lawyers who are sole practitioners or in small firms (they amaze me by their ability to do everything from divorces to slip-and-fall cases to estate planning) will find this book a useful reference when it's time to get down to basics. The practice pointers alone make it worth having on hand.

And, importantly, where a neighbor tries some mischief (like turning a hobby of breeding dogs into a commercial kennel), you will know how to defend your rights. Just as you can greatly increase your property's value, your neighbors can practically wipe you out by doing something bad with their property. No one wants to live next door to a _____ (you fill in the blank). What are you going to do when the kids next door jack up their cars and leave them on concrete blocks in various states of disrepair? What are you going to do when the accountant across the street starts meeting clients at his home office, leaving cars stacked up and down the street? What are going to do if you own an apartment building and the landlord behind you abandons her building? This book gives answers and strategies for dealing with such problems.

After publishing 175 professional articles, coediting one book, and coauthoring another, I realized that professional planners and lawyers had plenty of good advice and information available, but you, the homeowner, the real estate investor, the local planning commissioner and business entrepreneur, had been offered nothing.

So I jumped at the chance to write about what I have learned, much of it the hard way, in zoning wars over almost three decades. My reward will be to show up at a hearing and see you or others using this book to win at zoning.

How to Use This Book

If you have a couple of evenings to spare, you may wish to read this book from cover to cover. I have written it as I teach my courses to planners, developers, public officials, and law students. We start with the vocabulary of land-use law, discuss strategies for success, and follow with tactics and techniques for getting through the process.

However, I also welcome you to use the table of contents at the front and the index in the back to jump right to a hot topic. If you have a hearing ahead of you tomorrow night, you can skip right to that subject and attack it first. Many of your specific problems can be handled this way in short order.

Excuse the Warnings, But . . .

I'm a lawyer, so you know what I must tell you. First, what I write here has nothing to do with my clients or those of my law firm, past, present, or future. Don't think that you can jump up at a hearing where I'm representing a client and say something like George C. Scott did when playing Patton in the movie by the same name as he stood on the edge of the desert contemplating his battle with Rommel: "Dwight, you magnificent bastard, I read your book!" Besides, this book is more about strategies and tactics than about the substance of land-use law. For the substance, read my other books and articles.

And, of course, I'm not your lawyer; I'm just an author writing about a subject for general background. In most land-use cases, a property owner will benefit from consulting with a lawyer. Talk to one. Hire a professional planner, engineer, or environmental consultant as well. They can advise you on whether you need their help or not. Many times, after I review a case, I tell people that they can probably handle it on their own, but they can call me if they run into trouble. Other times, I will see a serious problem that they had blithely glossed over or missed entirely. While many land-use problems can be fixed through a second or third application, in some cases, you have only one shot—for example, when the town is in the process of changing its regulations and you have a pending application. In those cases, get professional help—don't blow your last chance at saving your property rights because you want to save some money at the wrong time.

I am not giving legal advice in this book, and I am not your lawyer. You need to understand that the law varies from state to state and from municipality to municipality, and that land-use cases are characteristically fact-driven. The facts of your particular property often determine the outcome. In that regard, by the way, question lawyers or planners who say that they can handle your case without seeing the property. I don't take a case or allow my people to work on one without walking the property. The site speaks to us in ways that nothing else can.

Finally, the many cases I comment on, among the thousands in which I have been involved, will not be traceable to any geographic area or particular parties because I have "dithered" the facts, changing irrelevant portions or combining aspects of several matters to completely obscure the actual case. In no event has any part of these case examples included anything that is not a matter of public record. That is indeed one of the unique attributes of zoning cases—they are profoundly public in almost every respect.

PART I

WHAT IS ZONING AND LAND-USE LAW?

Chapter 1

The Importance of Zoning in Creating and Protecting the Value of Real Estate

Zoning is the public regulation of land use. Local governments—villages, towns, cities, and counties—adopt zoning to control the types of uses and the bulk, density, and dimensions of those uses. The federal and state governments do not zone land, at least not as we know typical zoning, but what they say and do, as we shall see, can completely change the local zoning landscape. Through zoning, the government tells you what you can and cannot do with your own land. This directly affects the value and utility of your property.

Zoning regulations broadly categorize uses as residential, commercial, and industrial. Within these big three, there are many more detailed subcategories. Residential uses include single-family detached homes; duplexes or two-family homes; zero-lot-line homes, which are single-family homes with no side yards or only one side yard; multifamily homes, including townhouses and walk-up flats; mobile home parks; and apartment buildings.

There are as many possible categories as there are types of homes. The same goes for commercial uses, which range from small retail shops to warehouse stores that have floor plates of three acres or more. The variety of types and definitions is dizzying, even for the professionals. When writing regulations for local governments, it is best to concentrate on the definitions. Much of the law of zoning is simply in the definitions: how we choose and describe what is in and what is out.

To give you an idea of how definitions can rule the day, consider the movement to zone away fast-food chain restaurants. Some towns, in the belief that this is not a good use, have simply banned all formula restaurants, generally defined as restaurants with set architecture and a set menu that have more than a small number of outlets, say 10. You could have paid big money for a great site at a prime intersection for your national franchise fast-food restaurant and then have the zoning rug yanked out from underneath you with the adoption of a prohibition on formula restaurants. Watch out for those definitions!

In addition to the type of use, zoning regulates how intensively you can use your land. The regulation you probably are most familiar with is that of lot size. If you are in a one-acre residential zone, you need to have at least one acre to build one house. My guess is that you don't know how many square feet there are in an acre. Many of my land-use law students don't. It is 43,560 square feet. Now here's the curious part: No one else seems able to remember that odd number, so planners have come up with a little shortcut called the "zoning acre." That's right; many towns call an acre a nice, round 40,000 square feet so that no one has to remember the rest of it. I've had several cases where by designing the lots exactly to one "zoning" acre of 40,000 square feet, or one-half acre at 20,000 square feet, or whatever the lot size is, I have had enough land left over to make an additional lot. If you do the arithmetic, for every 12 lots at

40,000 square feet, you will get 1 extra lot free—that's found money, just like someone gave you land.

Other dimensional regulations include front-yard setbacks and side-yard setbacks—how far back from the lot line your building must be. Watch out for overhangs. Believe it or not, in most towns a bay window jutting out from the side of a house may be an illegal encroachment into the side yard if the foundation is right on the setback line. In a recent case, a homeowner had to remove a second-floor addition that projected into the side yard, even though it was built totally in the air without touching the ground.

What is a "structure," for purposes of determining what you can build where on your lot, can be found—you guessed it—in how a structure is defined. A gravel walkway is seldom a structure, but a walkway of poured concrete may be, and a slightly elevated wooden deck usually is. Sometimes you will find that the definitions point the way to how you can design your project to maximize the use of the land. A stone patio may be perfectly legal and serve your purposes just as well as a wooden deck in exactly the same spot would.

Dimensional limitations always include height and sometimes bulk. Height is expressed in feet above the ground or stories. For a house, the limitation is likely to be 35 feet or 3 1/2 stories. The fun begins when you try to figure out what is the ground and what is the top. If the ground is rolling or sloped, where do you take the measurement? It depends on (here we go again) the definitions.

Most regulations measure height from the ground to the top of the structure, of course, but where is the top? Sometimes it is the average height between the gable and a peak. More often than not, antennas, weathervanes, parapets (as compared with paralegals), cupolas, and chimneys are exempt. A friend added a lighthouse-like cupola to the top of his beach house, and a fight ensued over a flagpole at the peak. Was it exempt or not? The solution by this architect owner was to have a flagpole that slid down into the cupola. I guess he hoisted the pole when the zoning enforcement officer wasn't in the neighborhood.

This silliness abounds. When my ski house in Vermont was finished, the builder commented that by his measurement it was 38 feet high. One might dispute that statement, as it is on a steeply sloping lot with a walk-out at the front of the basement level and with the rear of the house buried in the hillside. Technically, by some measure, it might be in violation of the 35-foot limitation. (Don't turn me in for some bounty—I'll claim that the statute of limitations has expired.)

If you had that situation, what would you do? One lesson you will see repeatedly in this book is that with zoning there are many ways to get at most problems. With the too-tall house, I would ask a client in this pickle, "Well, as an experienced zoning lawyer, I see you have two choices: lower the roof or raise the ground." "Whaaat," the client would yelp. "You fool, I can't cut off the top of my house." So the answer is simple: You add three feet of fill around the house. Sounds crazy, but it works. Actually, as we shall see, there are many other ways of fixing a problem of non-compliance.

Sometimes the absolute size of a building is controlled. One way of limiting size is a regulation called a "square on the lot." This requires a minimum square or rectangle on a lot to make sure there is enough developable land on even the most oddly shaped lots. That square might be 100 feet by 100 feet, so it does little to control the maximum size. Such a square yields 10,000 square feet, a very large house.

To stop so-called McMansions, those really big houses on really small lots in older quaint neighborhoods, many towns have adopted maximum floor area restrictions and other controls. Pity the person who buys an expensive lot with a run-down house on it and plans to scrape off that house and build a starter palace, only to lose the right to do so with the adoption of an antimansion regulation. Watch out for changes that may reduce or wipe out the value of your property, especially when you haven't "vested" or legally locked in your right to develop by getting approvals or by starting construction. Vesting rules vary from state to state. In some states, for some types of development, it is enough that you have filed an application. If the regulations are changed after you submit your application, you can still build under the old regulations if your application is approved. Sometimes vesting does not occur until you have an approval; that is, right up to the time you get your approval, the local government can yank the zoning rug out from underneath you by changing the zoning.

The most common rule of vesting is "substantial construction in reliance upon a validly issued building permit." This means that you have to do some major work on the site, such as pouring concrete foundation footings, before your rights in that construction are vested against any subsequent changes in zoning. There have been so many instances of developers getting some substantial construction in the ground at the last minute that they have been given a special name, "midnight footings cases," suggesting that developers pour concrete in the dark of the night to get vested rights.

We had a case once where we were afraid this might happen. We were representing a neighborhood group that was opposing a small commercial development in a well-to-do rural town. We told the clients to keep an eye out for any construction activity on the site. On a Saturday morning, we received a frantic call that workers with a backhoe were on the property digging what appeared to be holes for foundations. We attempted unsuccessfully to reach the lawyer on the other side because he had promised to notify us before construction began. Eventually we found a judge, who happened to be working in his vegetable garden that morning. We got an order from him stopping the construction. Shortly thereafter, the lawyer on the other side returned our call and informed us that his client was merely transplanting some spruce trees. I know this all sounds like a tempest in a teapot. But, given the status of the case, with a zoning application pending and an amendment to the regulations that would stop the project under consideration, the potential construction of substantial improvements in reliance on the legally issued building permit was of prime importance. From the position of the neighborhood group, any vesting had to be stopped.

Another popular measure to control density for many types of buildings is the floor area ratio (FAR). This is not as technical as it sounds. With a one-acre lot, one of those zoning acre 40,000-square-foot types, with a FAR of 1.0, you can build 1 square foot of building floor area for each square foot of lot area. Thus, on a 40,000-square-foot lot, you could build 40,000 square feet of building. It could be on one level, but that might not work if you need drives and parking. It could be 20,000 square feet on each of two floors or 10,000 on each of four floors. A FAR of 0.5 would yield a total of 20,000 square feet of building per acre. A FAR of 2.0 would give you—you got it—80,000 square feet of building.

Do you see an emerging principle here? Small changes in somewhat innocuous controls or standards can yield large differences in development potential and value. That is the key to making money with zoning—finding ways to work within existing regulations to maximize the development of your land.

Watch out for a couple of other density and dimensional controls. There are open space ratios that specify the amount of open space on a lot that must be preserved. For example, an open space ratio of 0.5 would require that you leave half of the lot as open space. This open space may not have to be contiguous space—it could be fragmented with part on one portion of the lot and the remainder elsewhere on the lot. And, as you might imagine, when we talk about restrictive controls, we are always drawn back to definitions. In the case of open space ratios, we need to ask what counts as open space. Sometimes a stone patio or even a paved driveway can count as part of the open space; other times these things may not count.

A related regulation is the lot area coverage ratio, which is, as the name suggests, simply the ratio of the coverage of structures on a lot to the total lot area. Again, you need to know what counts as a structure for lot coverage purposes. We have been forced to research this issue so many times that it has become a running joke in our office.

I remember as a first-year lawyer spending many hours digging through law reporters (before computer research) trying to determine what is and what is not a structure. You would be surprised at what counts and what doesn't. A flagpole is actually a structure in most states, but, obviously, it doesn't use up much of your coverage ratio. An overhanging awning over your back door that protects you from the weather as you enter your home might count toward your lot coverage, even though it is not attached to the ground. I can't imagine how this issue ever became a law case, but there is one instance where a court held that a "locomotive undergoing repair" was not a structure.

I recently purchased a 1916 New York Central caboose to restore and use as a guest house at my home in Vermont. We put a section of track on the property and trucked the caboose there. My builder asked if I had checked the side-yard setback requirements, and I glibly suggested that because the caboose was "rolling stock," it should not be counted as a structure. He had a more practical view and went to the zoning enforcement officer to make sure we located the caboose outside the side-yard setback. This is one of those instances where common sense transcends legal technicalities.

Making and Losing Money with Zoning

This introductory discussion about how zoning works and what is found in a typical zoning ordinance suggests some of the ways in which money can be made and lost through zoning. A modest change in density can result in large changes in value. If you can change the zoning in your one-acre residential zone from that one acre per lot to three-quarters of an acre per lot, just a 25 percent reduction in size, you can increase the number of lots from the same area of land by one-third. That's right, with this modest change, you can increase the development potential of your land by fully one-third. The cost of development generally will not increase with an increase in the number of lots in the same parcel because the fixed costs, such as the length of road and utilities, do not change. These "new" lots, therefore, come with "free" utilities and are pure profit.

Even a slight change in use classification can yield great new value. Suppose you own a small block of stores in the center of town that is zoned for traditional retail uses. If you can get the use classification amended to allow a somewhat more intensive use, such as medical offices, you can greatly increase the rent you command for those very same buildings.

Many old buildings do not conform to existing regulations. These uses of buildings and land are called *nonconforming* uses. Regulations usually prohibit their enlargement. If you are a factory owner, you could increase your production and profit if you could expand your building on that site, instead of going to the great expense of relocating to a larger facility elsewhere. Using some of the techniques explained in this book, you as the factory owner may be able to expand the building regardless of the apparent limitations of the local law. One approach would be to amend the zoning ordinance to allow a modest expansion by special permit to existing industrial facilities constructed before a certain date (conveniently, a date not long after the time your building was built). Another approach might be to request a variance, claiming a "practical difficulty and unnecessary hardship" based on the fact that the building was built many years before, long before adoption of the existing regulations.

It may be the lot coverage ratio or the open space ratio that prevents you as the owner of an existing manufacturing plant from expanding that facility. A modest change in one or both of those ratios, limited to a small subset of buildings (which, of course, would include your building), could be all that would be necessary to allow you to expand in place, rather than moving elsewhere. The local zoning scheme would not be substantially or adversely changed, and you will keep money in your pocket.

Just as you can create value through zoning strategies, a neighbor can wipe you out and make your property virtually useless, all within the limits of the law and local zoning regulations. One of the more universal examples of this type of unfortunate happenstance is the group of college students who take over a single-family home. While the typical definition of a family often prohibits a group of college students from moving into a neighborhood, that is not always the case. We pejoratively refer to this living arrangement as "eight guys, four cars, and two kegs." A group of college students can always outbid a traditional family for rent, and their activities in most cases are a blighting influence on the immediate neighbors.

I had one interesting case in a rather upscale rural town involving a pilot who decided, believe it or not, that he would just build his own little private airfield in his backyard. Having small planes buzzing in and out disrupted the neighbors, who kept horses. I represented the town, and we eventually resolved the case, but only after protracted litigation. The controversy could have been avoided in the first instance if someone had thought to prohibit airfields and landing areas in the rural district. We've seen this problem repeated in many other places with private helicopters.

As with most zoning problems, an ounce of prevention is worth a pound of cure.

There are also numerous cases across the country of agricultural operations, apparently legal under the existing zoning, that have made surrounding residential properties unusable because of the dust and smells of normal farming. "Normal" farming today may be the equivalent of heavy industry. A "mega-hog farm" with thousands of pigs, which the federal government refers to as a "concentrated animal feeding operation (CAFO)," bears no resemblance whatsoever to the traditional family farm we see at the beginning of *The Wizard of Oz*.

There is a legal doctrine called "coming to the nuisance" that in its simplest expression says that someone who moves close to something that is a potential nuisance should not be allowed to complain. This doctrine has come to be out of favor, and we are seeing an increasing number of cases in which disputes arise over incompatible uses in close proximity to each other.

To protect your property value, you must be ever vigilant about what your neighbors are doing. You should make sure that your local regulations require written notice to abutting property owners by certified mail, return receipt requested. This will save you from having to read the fine-print public notices in the local newspaper every day or every week to learn what your neighbors may be up to.

The title insurance policy on your property does not protect you in terms of either the zoning for your own parcel or changes in the zoning on surrounding parcels. You need to make sure before you buy property that you understand exactly what the zoning allows and prohibits. You need to consider asking your local zoning authority for reasonable and modest amendments to the regulations that will protect you from detrimental neighbors. Do the local zoning regulations prohibit storing unregistered cars on residential properties? Can someone park a derelict 40-foot wooden boat in the side yard and cover it with a huge plastic tarp—spending 10 years preparing it for a world cruise and, of course, never finishing the project?

I have a friend who erected a large yurt (a round, tent-like fabric enclosure over a wooden frame) in his yard, without the benefit of any building permit or zoning approval, so that he and his friends could meditate together. I'm not sure that a yurt will enhance property values in his neighborhood. The plain fact is, there are more bad things that your neighbors can do than you could possibly imagine.

One of the more restrictive forms of regulation is one that expressly provides that any use that is not expressly permitted is expressly prohibited. (I know that's a lot of "expressly's" in one sentence, but sometimes that is exactly what it takes to get the job done.) On the side of creating value, regulations of this type may be inhibitive, but in terms of protecting your property value from a lot of people who do strange things, they may be just what you need.

Many new residential developments have added another layer of protection with covenants and restrictions on their properties by mutual agreement. These covenants and restrictions are prepared by the developer and declared before the lots are first sold. While it may be difficult, it is indeed possible for you to get together with your neighbors and add these restrictions to existing properties. You might want to look into adopting your own controls for your neighborhood regarding the design of buildings and guidelines for appearance, such as paint color and the maintenance of landscaped buffers. The covenants and restrictions in our neighborhood, for example, include a requirement that the homes be of "colonial or traditional architecture," that they be painted in "colonial or earth tone" colors, that clothes not be hung outside, and that the cars be parked in the garages and not left out in the driveways. The company that laid out the subdivision had to approve the designs of the independently constructed homes and the landscape plans. The objective was to create a neighborhood of compatible homes. In the parlance of planning terminology, we refer to these types of controls as ones intended to prevent "negative externalities." The covenants and restrictions prevent a property owner from doing something that would have an adverse effect on abutting and nearby properties.

You can do a lot more with private covenants and restrictions than the government can do with public regulation because private restrictions are not subject to most constitutional protections.

For example, it is unlikely that the government could impose a restriction prohibiting dogs, or dogs over a certain size, in a residential neighborhood, but there are numerous developments that do just that through private covenants and easements. One of the oddest examples of this comes up in the conversion of existing apartment buildings to condominiums, where we have included, at the developer's request, "dog amortization" provisions. Try to guess what this means. *Amortization* means elimination over time, and "dog amortization" provisions usually state that a tenant who purchases his or her apartment as a condominium unit following the conversion can keep a dog that he or she had at the time of conversion, but that when the dog dies, it cannot be replaced. These provisions eliminate dogs in a project over time.

No government is going to have such a law because it would be politically impossible (just imagine someone proposing such a regulation!) and probably indefensible as a matter of statutory and constitutional law. But developers and homeowners who have decided that they don't want large dogs or any dogs in their neighborhoods can agree by private covenant and restriction to have their neighborhoods without dogs or as they want them. Some restrictions, though, even by private agreement, are illegal. These are racial, ethnic, and religious restrictions and restrictions on other protected classes, such as persons who are protected under the Americans with Disabilities Act.

Probably the worst thing that can happen to you in terms of losing the value in your property is not to understand what the zoning allows and to buy in reliance on assumptions that turn out to be wrong. The most tragic case in my entire career involved a family that had spent its life savings on a combined residential and commercial operation. (I'll speak of the case in general terms, even though it was 20 years ago, to protect the identity of the family.) Shortly after they moved in and continued that commercial operation just as the prior owner had operated it, the zoning enforcement officer issued a cease and desist order, shutting the commercial operation down.

Their lawyer at the time chose to sue the real estate broker and the seller for misrepresentation when he should have taken a much more active approach and attempted to get the zoning changed to allow the commercial use, which both the seller and the new buyer had assumed was legal. The case against the broker and the seller ran on for more than a year, and the property fell into foreclosure because the family had been dependent on the commercial operation to generate enough income to pay a portion of the mortgage.

I was eventually retained to try to solve the problem. I went to the local zoning authority, which quickly amended the regulations to allow the commercial venture. This was a simple, expedient, and straightforward resolution. The local zoning board was sympathetic to the family.

This was a small town, and the chairman of the board was a high school teacher who had the family's only child as a student. The teacher had noted a decline in the child's performance at school and suspected some problem at home, but no one had told him that it was a matter of interpreting the zoning regulations.

Once he heard what the problem was, he was quick to bring a resolution to help the family.

Regrettably, it was too late. By the time we achieved this quick fix, the family was so far in arrears on the mortgage that it lost the property (and its life savings just as the father was reaching retirement age). The family left the area, and I don't know what happened to these people in the end. It continues to trouble me two decades later that those who were supposed to be helping the family could not see their way through to a simple solution.

Let me say this again: One of the keys to success in the zoning game is understanding that there are almost always several ways to address a problem. The challenge for anyone in this business is to have a sufficient command of available opportunities to orchestrate an approach that yields an optimum result quickly. This type of tragedy should never have happened. It was entirely avoidable, or at least readily correctable.

The people involved in this transaction should have looked at the zoning more carefully before the purchase was completed. The lawyer who was first retained to represent them once they discovered the problem also represented them in the closing. He should have attempted to fix the zoning rather than take the stereotypical lawyer's approach of suing everybody in sight for damages, without even attempting to solve the underlying zoning problem.

Chapter 2

Zoning as Part of the Larger Regulatory Environment

Don't Get Too Enamored with Public Regulation

Make no mistake about it, public regulation, including zoning, has a profound impact on the use and value of your property. However, public regulation is just one of several factors controlling the use of land and determining its value.

In Chapter 1, we noted how important private covenants and restrictions can be in regulating the use of land. Some would argue that private restrictions have now assumed the primary role in the regulation of land use, but I would not agree, although private restrictions have become increasingly important, and their reach will continue to expand.

Planners would like to think that we start with a plan and adopt regulations based on it. Then, development consistent with both the plan and the regulations should somehow occur. That indeed is the rational planning model, but the plain fact is, it doesn't usually work in that pure form.

All the plans and regulations in the world cannot change some greater determinants of how land will be used. First and foremost is the market. If the private market for real estate will not support a particular form of development, it won't happen. Often developers of large projects will come to me and ask what the plans and regulations allow them to do with their property. More often than not, I tell them to design the best project they can consistent with the market. Then we will look at the plans and the regulations and determine whether we need to amend the plans to permit the project. In the end, every project must be marketable, profitable, and approvable.

The second major determinant of how the land will be developed is infrastructure. *Infrastructure* is an overused word that includes all of the utilities and physical support systems for development. When we speak of infrastructure, we include roads, water, sewers, sanitary sewers, storm-water drainage, public services (fire, police, and emergency services), schools, and even the government. Assuming that there is a market, if all the utilities are there and you have a good local government, the development will come.

Jokingly, I say that when I have dinner with my planner friends, we ultimately end up talking about sanitary sewers by the time we reach the dessert course. That really happens in many instances, because sewers and water, and to some extent roads, ultimately determine the development capacity of property. Water is available in many areas, and once sewers go in, the natural constraints on the ability of soil to absorb the septic disposal are no longer a factor, and so development can go to just about any density.

It is the primacy of infrastructure as a determinant of development that leads me to tell planners that they should concentrate their efforts at the local level on capital improvement programming. Capital improvement programming is a form of planning that looks at all of the capital (physical) improvements for infrastructure and then extends and expands the capacity of those improvements in an orderly fashion so that the growth is directed where it should be, not where it happens to be today by reason of "accident," such as the extension of a sewer main along the frontage of some prime agricultural land.

Does this mean that I think that planning is unimportant? No. Planning is essential. We need to plan now for future generations. We must plan when the market fails us, and we must plan so that development doesn't occur as a haphazard result of infrastructure being placed without regard for the inevitable development that follows.

Planning addresses the needs of future generations not yet born. The market generally will never comprehend that time horizon. Developers need to maximize their return today, this year, or within the next several years. We should not expect them to be thinking about the effect of their developments 50 or 100 years hence. I had the remarkable experience of assisting, as a consultant, on the creation of the plan and regulations for the 4,500 acres around the new Denver International Airport. The plan for that area and the regulations implementing the plan anticipated a build-out of about 100 years. It is at that scale and with that long-term horizon that planning proves most beneficial.

Planning is also essential for locating infrastructure in the right places so that we get the right development at the right time.

The important point to remember, however, is that public planning and public regulation by themselves are not necessarily the main drivers of development. I would not want you as a property owner to think that you can do everything with zoning—you can't.

Other Regulations at the Local Level

You should expect to encounter many regulations other than zoning at the local level. Just as in the old adage that "a chain is only as strong as its weakest link," you won't be able to undertake your project unless you have each and every one of the locally required permits, as well as state and federal approvals.

Here's a short list of some of the types of local regulations you are likely to find.

Subdivision

Subdivision regulations control the division of land. They are designed to do two things: (1) ensure that there is adequate infrastructure and access to parcels of land before they are sold, and (2) create clear titles to land. Subdivision regulations generally do not control the use of land and seldom control the dimensions of a lot beyond requiring some minimum developable area or access to a public street. The subdivision regulations are guided in part by the zoning regulations, which ultimately set minimum lot area, frontage, and other dimensional standards.

The land developer must take care not to paint herself into a corner by carving off lots along road frontage, only to find that she has undevelopable land to the rear. Rear land may be developed by creating interior lots, which are sometimes called "flag" lots because in shape they resemble a flag, with the pole being the driveway access to the rear portion, the developable area of the lot, which is in the shape of a rectangle. These rear lots are often undesirable in terms of protecting privacy because the front yard of the rear lot looks into the rear yard of a lot in front of it. Such lots are somewhat disfavored in planning and are sometimes derisively called "pork chop" lots, again playing on the shape.

The most egregious use of the rear-lot layout that I ever saw was a project in Otis, Massachusetts, where the developer laid out very narrow lots—50 feet wide for most of the length until they widened at the lakefront, if I remember correctly—with some of them a mile long. The objective was to gain access to a public street and thereby avoid formal subdivision approval based on the law in Massachusetts at the time. Those regulations have since changed, largely as a result of this type of abuse and this particular notorious project. The larger developable portions of the lots were located around a pond with a rudimentary road not built to town standards. The *Boston Globe* published an editorial critical of the development in which it referred to the layout as "rat tail lots." It doesn't get any more disparaging than that.

Floodplain and Wetlands Approval

Many, but by no means all, local jurisdictions have some type of wetlands approval. At the very least, every municipality has some type of floodplain regulation, either at the local or at the county level. You can't build in a floodway—where the water actually flows—and you are limited in what you can build in a floodplain, which is usually defined as the elevation flooded during a 100-year storm. A 100-year storm is one that occurs on average, statistically, every 100 years. Because of upland development, however, many jurisdictions have experienced 100-year, and greater, floods on a far more frequent basis. The developer can do some limited filling and some construction within the 100-year floodplain if there is little or no impact on flood height, if the water will flow freely under and around the structures, and if there are adequate escape routes at or above the 100-year flood elevation.

Anyone who is buying or developing property should check the Flood Insurance Rate Maps published by the Federal Emergency Management Agency under the National Flood Insurance Program. These maps show the 100-year floodplain and the floodways. As with all things regulatory, take extra care to make sure you have the most recent maps.

If you don't like what you see on the map, consult a qualified engineer. Often, the maps can be refined through a petitioning process, and you can create additional developable land by getting portions of your property out of the 100-year floodplain. Sometimes that requires only an engineering study and a petition to amend the map. Sometimes it requires some construction, as in the case where we won approval for a super-regional shopping mall project that discharged its storm water to a stream, and the lots for a large number of homes were partially within the 100-year floodplain. By changing the culverts (large drainage pipes crossing under the road) and channelizing the stream at some locations, our engineers were able to demonstrate to the Federal Emergency Management Agency that the 100-year floodplain would be reduced because the water could pass through the area more freely. As a consequence, over 100 lots were taken out of the floodplain, substantially reducing the risk of flooding for those properties and thereby increasing public safety and enhancing property values. You can do the same thing on a lesser scale, with even a single lot, if you look carefully at the Flood Insurance Rate Map and consult a qualified engineer.

Under the National Flood Insurance Program, insurance is available to properties that include areas within the 100-year floodplain. You may have purchased an existing property with improvements in the floodplain, and the best and least expensive flood insurance available (and sometimes the only flood insurance available) is through this program. I know one riverfront restaurant that is in the 100-year floodplain, and has been since long before the National Flood Insurance Program, which is designed to minimize damage from floods by the adoption of mandatory flood damage prevention regulations. By my reckoning, about every five or six years, the first floor of this restaurant is flooded out when the river goes above flood stage. And each time the federal government steps up and pays for the restoration of the restaurant. Because the flood insurance program allows properties like this to be rebuilt, it is much maligned by those who would prefer to have the portions of properties that are below the 100-year flood elevation undeveloped. The program does include required relocation in some circumstances. Anyone buying or owning property with structures below the 100-year flood elevation should keep in mind that these properties will be periodically flooded. If history teaches us anything, we should also expect public regulation to get tougher and eventually require that some improvements be relocated to upland areas, which may not be physically possible on some parcels.

In addition to floodplains, local governments often regulate wetlands. Wetlands are defined differently at the federal level from the way they are defined in some states, so we cannot provide a single definition that is valid everywhere. Typically, wetlands are defined in terms of being wet part of the time. Certainly, a pond or a stream would be a wetland or watercourse. Wetlands are also defined by poorly drained soils, which tend to be mucky and on which water will pond during a heavy storm. A qualified soils scientist, using an auger (a digging device), can pull up samples of soil and then determine the soil type and whether it is a poorly drained soil or not. Wetlands are also sometimes defined in part by whether they support wetland-type plants, such as red maples and skunk cabbage.

You want to know whether your property has wetlands or not because developing in wetlands may be physically impossible or expensive. You cannot locate septic systems in wetlands without considerable extra expense to bring in permeable soils to create an adequate leaching field so that the underground pipes can pass the effluent into the soil. Buildings may require pilings driven deep through the spongy soils to firm ground below. Wetland soils are not good for lawns either, so often these soils have to be excavated and topsoil has to be brought in.

More importantly, local regulations may simply prohibit or strongly discourage development in wetlands. Local laws may also require a buffer area around wetlands under the theory that activities that occur upland of the wetlands could still have an impact on them through surface flows. For example, if you apply excessive amounts of herbicide to your lawn 50 feet away from a wetland, the herbicide is likely to be carried along the surface and into the wetland, where it will have an adverse effect.

You should start by inquiring whether there are wetlands regulations. If there are such regulations and you suspect that you may have wetlands on your property, you should hire a qualified soils scientist who is an environmental professional with experience in wetlands delineation to "flag" the wetlands. The wetlands professional will walk your property, evaluate the plants, dig up cores of soil with an auger, and then place tiny flags on wires into the ground (thus the term *flagging*) identifying the edge of the wetlands. Your surveyor can then survey the location of all those flags and put them on a map. From there, you can determine what buffer you need to have in order to comply with local regulations or to ensure that your development activity does not have an adverse impact on the wetland system.

Even the toughest wetlands regulations systems are licensing regulations; they do not absolutely prohibit development in wetlands, but they do require you to go through a process of local review and approval. Wetlands regulation has become tougher and tougher each year over the last quarter century, and if you have wetlands, you should reasonably expect that you're not going to be building on them, except for the minimal encroachments necessary to make reasonable use of your property. Those minimal encroachments, which are routinely approved, include road crossings in areas where the wetlands are narrow, and some clearing and revegetation in and around development sites. You might also get permission to use portions of the wetlands for storm-water retention and detention so that runoff from the site does not damage properties downstream or flood out the areas you are developing.

If your wetlands expert tells you that you have a "vernal pool," sit up and pay attention! A vernal pool is a special type of wetland system that supports certain types of species not found in any other habitat, such as wood frogs, fairy shrimp, and salamanders. These pools are vernal in that they emerge in the springtime, have standing water in them until the early summer, and then dry up. As a consequence, these pools cannot support fish, and the fish are not there to eat the eggs of the salamanders and other species that thrive in these environments.

Vernal pools do not necessarily contain endangered species, but these pools are an uncommon type of wetland system, and their preservation has become increasingly important. Furthermore, to protect a vernal pool habitat, it is often necessary to protect large areas of upland, perhaps a buffer of as much as 300 to 500 feet for three-quarters of the way or more around the vernal pool. We have even seen instances where the upland habitats of the salamanders, which travel between the upland and the vernal pools at different points in their life cycle, were located some 1,200 feet or more away from the vernal pool, necessitating the preservation of the corridor between the upland habitat and the vernal pool. You can lose development of substantial areas through the need to preserve this unique type of habitat.

Traffic Regulation

Many local governments have a traffic authority, sometimes the police chief, who is responsible for making sure that there is safe and convenient access to and from your property. The traffic authority will want to review your traffic report, which will describe the number of trips to and from your proposed project at each hour throughout the day. This person will be especially interested in knowing what the peak-hour (that one hour during the day when the number of trips is the largest) traffic counts are and whether the road system is capable of handling the traffic.

The level of traffic is measured in terms of levels of service. The levels of service (LOS) are rated from A to F, but not like a report card. A LOS of A means that the traffic is unimpeded and free-flowing, every driver's dream. The respectable LOS of C is normal heavy traffic, and a LOS of D is still acceptable, although a driver will be stuck at a traffic signal through at least one and maybe two cycles of the light before being able to continue. A LOS of F means that the traffic system has failed. This is your basic gridlock situation, in which traffic barely flows and road rage erupts. There are some intersections that can never be improved beyond a LOS of F, and this is an undesirable situation.

Most professional engineers can handle some traffic review, but for any significant development project, you're going to want to have a qualified traffic engineer.

Opposition groups can count cars just as well as a traffic engineer. Their evidence is admissible nearly all of the time and is just as legally acceptable as that of the traffic engineer, at least as to numbers of cars and the accident history of a roadway.

Local knowledge can be especially probative. I once had a residential subdivision where several driveways were clustered together to get a single access point out onto a road. The road had a sharp horizontal curve, making it difficult to see around the corner. We call this a *horizontal alignment problem*. When you can't see over the top of a hill because it is steep and the angle at the top is sharp, this is called a *vertical sight line* problem. I was trying to explain to a local planning commission the need to join the driveways to provide safe access to the road. An affable, older commissioner asked if I meant down on the Old Post Road. When I said that was the area, he replied, "Oh, you mean dead man's curve." He knew exactly what the problem was, and we got our approval.

The traffic engineer provides a level of expertise on the design of road systems and the integration of traffic signals that goes beyond merely counting cars. It is an art and a science to forecast the number of trips to and from a development site and to identify the distribution of those trips. Sometimes you just can't do without a professional traffic engineer.

I have never seen a project for which permission was ultimately denied because of traffic. Traffic is often a major issue and the subject of much debate at public hearings, but in the end most bad traffic situations can be improved by road widening, the addition of turning lanes, and signalization. In one particularly tough situation, our client agreed to run shuttle buses during the holiday season to relieve some of the congestion. The developer also purchased a vacant property across the street from the shopping center that was potentially a high-traffic-generating bank site and permanently preserved it as open space. This removed a substantial number of potential cars from the roadway system permanently. The developer also created overflow parking in grassy areas with a system called "reinforced turf," which looks like a lawn but has the bearing capacity of asphalt. It was a great solution to the seasonal parking needs of the shopping center.

Design Review

Many local governments have a process of design review. The boards are often advisory only; that is, they do not have final decision-making authority that can result in a denial of a project, but they advise some other decision maker, such as the planning board or council. Some developers dislike design review boards because they don't like the idea of a board telling them what they can or should do with their project. Most design review boards have one or more architects and other design professionals. Our experience is that if they are approached early on and have a chance to offer suggestions before much time and money has been spent on the design of a project, they can assist in optimizing the design and getting other local authorities to grant permits.

Historic District Review

Your local government may have a historic district or districts. In historic districts, the government regulates the appearance of buildings, usually the portions seen from a public way. You can't hang an air conditioner out a second-floor window on the street side of a building in a historic district without a review by the local historic district commission and the issuance of a certificate of appropriateness. You can't put up storm windows in most cases. In many instances, you can't even paint your house a new color without permission. We have seen cases involving just about everything you can imagine happening in a historic district and some that none of us could even dream up.

In one instance, a gentleman who owned a nondescript World War II–era Cape Cod house wanted to be added to the district (many people try to stay out of them) because he thought it would add value to his property—which it would. He got into the district. In another case, an enforcement action was started against a homeowner because he placed an acclaimed sculpture in this yard. In yet another case, the owner of a summer home battled over whether he should be able to put up glass windows on a screened porch. The Historic District Commission said that it would detract from the district and refused to issue a certificate of appropriateness. You certainly cannot add to your home or build a new house in a historic district without approval in most jurisdictions. That's right, in many historic districts, even new construction is completely controlled by a historic district commission.

State Permits

There are many types of state permits. They vary, as you can well imagine, from state to state, from project to project, and, of course, from time to time. Our discussion is necessarily limited, but it will give you a sense of what to expect.

Environmental Permits

The state environmental permitting process is parallel with and sometimes overlaps the local approval process. Some environmental permits are unique to the state level. They typically involve issues of regional and statewide concern.

If there's one permit that is most often overlooked, with the greatest adverse impact on project developers as a result, it is the National Pollutant Discharge Elimination System (NPDES) Section 401 Water Quality Certificate, a permit that is administered by the states, but is required under the federal Clean Water Act.

This permit is necessary for construction of all but the smallest projects and for the discharge of storm water. The developer generally cannot receive a local building permit without having the NPDES Section 401 in hand, and, tragically, some developers don't discover that they need it until they show up at the building official's office for a building permit. They then have to go back to the state to have the permit processed, which can take many months. One of our key pointers for anybody owning or developing property is to make contact with all of the potential federal, state, and local officials early on. In this case, contact with local and state officials would bring the need for this permit to the surface and give the developer time to get it.

Some states, New York and Massachusetts among them, have a comprehensive environmental review process at the state level for larger projects. Vermont has a process of regional reviews for larger projects. Florida reviews projects that have regional impact. Again, it is important to make contact with state officials at the outset and determine whether your project may require a comprehensive environmental review. If it does, you will begin with a somewhat cursory environmental impact assessment, which will attempt to scope out the extent of the review required. Then, under some state systems, you will go to a much more detailed and definitive environmental impact review. If you need this review and you don't get it, you may lose everything. We know of one project where the developer got bad advice on the need for a comprehensive state environmental review and went ahead with building a large store, only to have the neighborhood opposition drag the developer into court and get a court ruling that the building could not be constructed without the environmental review. The project was abandoned at a loss of several million dollars.

At the same time, there are instances where even though there may be opposition and claims that additional review is needed, the developer will decide to go forward. This will happen if the developer feels secure enough about the outcome, and if the rewards of proceeding outweigh the risks of having to stop the project later. One of our developer clients completed a $54 million project while the status of the permits was being challenged in court by an opposition group. Fortunately (for all of us!), our predictions about the outcome were accurate, and the building did not have to be torn down.

Required permits from traffic authorities are infrequently encountered at the local level but are almost always found in one form or another at the state level with most larger development projects. The usual statutory scheme is one in which larger projects are subjected to a state-level review, especially where there may be a direct or indirect impact on a state roadway system. Note the importance of identifying an "indirect" impact. Maybe your property is not on a state highway but is a couple of miles away from the highway. It may appear at first that the state might not regulate your development, but if your trip distribution is such that most of your traffic is going to go that two miles right to the state highway, you could have a regulated site. It is unlikely that the state would stop you from developing your property, but you may suffer the extraordinary expense of putting in a traffic signal, which the last time I looked was running at about $125,000 for the simplest and smallest system; adding two lanes to a road to the state highway; or building a new interstate interchange. Yes, I have seen a developer required to build an entire interchange to an interstate highway as a condition of approving the development. This type of exaction has been labeled by some courts as an "out-and-out plan of extortion," but in most circumstances the highway improvements undertaken by developers in furtherance of their projects are worth it because they enable shoppers or residents to get to and from the sites quickly and conveniently. An alternative to requiring one developer to make these physical improvements is to share the cost among several developers through impact fees, with each paying a pro rata share of the cost.

If you happen to be in a coastal state, you should be prepared for another massive layer of regulation under a coastal management act. You'll need to be concerned about tidal wetlands, dredging, and filling as well as about the navigational impacts of structures, such as docks and pilings for the support of buildings.

Some of the most controversial development cases arise in the coastal context. I can think of a couple of dozen notorious cases that have taken 20 years or more to be resolved. Anthony Palazzolo of Westerly, Rhode Island, started attempting to develop his coastal property more than 30 years ago. His case, which involves the filling of tidal wetlands, ultimately made its way to the U.S. Supreme Court, and as I'm writing this book, Tony is now 83 years old and is back in a trial court trying once again to either get approval to fill some tidal wetlands for development or be compensated by the government for being prohibited from doing so.

This is not to discourage people from buying properties with environmental restrictions, but it is noteworthy that the most intractable cases seem to have arisen in the coastal context. Watch out as well for the potential of overlapping jurisdictions. As we saw of the NPDES permits, and as we shall see further later, there are federal permit processes that are administered by the states. To some degree, there is also local jurisdiction over some of the same resources regulated by the state and federal governments, for example, wetlands.

If you have a coastal property, check for the 100-year flood elevation and look at the resource maps available from state authorities for the location of any protected plant species or organisms on the site. It is illegal even to cut some of the marsh grasses on your property without a permit. We had one client who removed some poison ivy from a coastal lot, only to end up in a controversy with the state because poison ivy was among the types of plant species listed as indicative of tidal wetlands. That surprised all of us.

Other Environmental Permits at the State Level

There are a host of other permits required from the state, too numerous to list. You may need an air quality permit, even for a furnace. It could be that the traffic coming to and going from your property will generate enough air pollution to require a permit. If there are potential archaeological resources on the site, you may need clearance from a state agency and, prior to that, a site investigation by a qualified archaeologist. Is there an airport nearby? If so, there may be restrictions on approach zones that will control the use or height of your buildings. Perhaps your property is located along a scenic corridor. If that is the case, you may need a permit from the regional authority in the state overseeing that "gateway" resource, such as a river or mountain pass. If your property has been contaminated by pollutants, which may not show up in a visual inspection or even with soils and water testing, it may be listed on a state registry and be subject to cleanup requirements. The subject of environmental remediation and the restoration of sites so that they may be reused (called "brownfields" development) is a major issue that is beyond the scope of this limited work.

Federal Regulation of Land Use

Federal zoning? You say you've never heard of such a thing? There is federal zoning, but it is not called that.

One exception might be the Coastal Zone Management Act, which requires a state to enact and administer regulations to protect the coastal zone. Even that is not viewed by most people as zoning, but rather as coastal area resource regulation. It may require a review of water-dependent uses to make sure the coast is not wasted on developments that don't need to be right on the water. How did all the waterfront restaurants get there? Some developers have argued that a restaurant may not be water-dependent but is "water-enhanced," meaning that people are willing to pay more for their dinners when they can dine with a water view. How is that for some nimble wordsmithing? This isn't really zoning, however, because beyond the issue of water-dependent uses, there is little use for regulation.

Coastal zone management does not regulate the bulk, area, and density usually found in zoning. It is, in essence, an overlay of federal controls designed to protect what is largely a federal resource.

Some people argue that NPDES regulation is largely a type of federal zoning because if you can restrict the discharge of storm water, you ultimately have some leverage over the type, intensity, and location of development. That argument is somewhat of a stretch. Without question, NPDES affects local development, but it is hardly zoning.

In at least two instances, federal law directly overrides local zoning and substitutes federal decision making for that of local authorities. This is federal zoning, plain and simple. One of those laws is the Fair Housing Amendments Act, which prohibits discrimination against certain protected individuals, largely those protected by the Americans with Disabilities Act. Local regulations cannot zone out certain protected classes of individuals, among them recovering alcoholics and substance abusers, the physically disabled, and the mentally retarded. The general rule is that group homes for such individuals must be allowed in single-family residential neighborhoods and elsewhere on the same terms as any other traditional family. Some federal courts have allowed restrictions on the numbers of people, and in some rare cases, federal courts have upheld local denials of group homes where there are compelling public health and safety concerns for the potential residents, such as inadequate road access. Nearly all of the cases, however, go for the protected classes of individuals.

This is clearly a federal override of local zoning, but Congress and our presidents have determined that it is of national importance to mainstream these individuals and the group households of these individuals in society. The most responsible approach to this override for local governments and for individual property owners is to zone land for such homes in advance, provide reasonable alternatives for their location within the community, and work constructively and cooperatively with the developers, owners, and operators of such group homes to find them good locations. With good design and responsible management, these group homes can blend seamlessly into the fabric of a traditional single-family community. The most significant danger is when there are large concentrations of such group homes in a small area. This stresses the existing neighborhood and detracts from the opportunities to mainstream the protected individuals.

Another important federal override, which is just as much federal zoning as the Fair Housing Amendments Act, is the Religious Land Use and Institutionalized Persons Act (RLUIPA, pronounced "ree-loop-a"). RLUIPA protects religious activities and institutionalized persons in their religious practices. We'll skip the latter category and look at the first.

The short version of RLUIPA is that a local government cannot unreasonably restrict the free exercise of religion. That's an oversimplification of the somewhat more complex law, but it's good enough for our purposes.

Suppose that a couple next door to you has decided to form a new religious order. Over the last six months, they have held prayer meetings in their home, with between three and seven other people coming to their house in three or four cars. You have not noticed the activity, and you would not have known anything about it had you not learned of your neighbors' interest in this new religious movement when talking with your neighbor while borrowing gasoline for your lawnmower.

Interest in this new sect has increased of late, and now prayer meetings are being held not only on Sunday morning, but also on Wednesday night. The number of members has increased to the point where around certain religious holidays there are 20 to 30 cars parked up and down the street and 30 to 50 people gathered in the home. Sometimes you can't even get in or out of your driveway, and you are worried for the safety of your children who ride their bicycles on the street. Fortunately, perhaps by divine intervention, there have been no accidents yet.

While you don't feel good about it, you call the zoning enforcement officer to ask if this is a permitted use. She comes by the next Wednesday evening and notices all of the cars and the activity. She talks with your neighbors and learns more about what they are doing. The zoning regulations do not allow a church in your residential zone, and she reluctantly warns your neighbors that they should stop having these large prayer meetings at their home. They tell the zoning enforcement officer that it is not for them to decide, that it is the decision of a higher power, and the meetings must continue. The zoning enforcement officer reluctantly issues a cease and desist order.

During the local administrative review of your neighbor's appeal of the zoning enforcement officer's order, there is much discussion about traffic and congestion on the street. Ultimately, after much wrangling, the local government upholds the zoning enforcement officer's decision and orders the activity to stop.

Previously, this would have been the end of the matter. In their appeal, your neighbors might have made a claim under the federal or state constitutions based on the free exercise of their religion, but it is unlikely that they would have gotten far with it. With RLUIPA on the scene, however, the outcome has changed dramatically. This hypothetical is based on a real case in which the neighbors who started a church in their home ultimately were successful. They were able to continue their services, because the local government did not show enough significant public health and safety concerns, such as traffic safety, to overcome the protections of RLUIPA.

As a property owner wanting to create value in your property, RLUIPA might be beneficial, as it might allow you to greatly intensify the use of your property even where the local zoning does not authorize it, such as by converting a home or a storefront to a church. The cases we've seen so far haven't arisen that way, however; they are more like this hypothetical, where they start from small gatherings and grow through the success of the religion. You might make money by establishing group homes under the protections of the Fair Housing Amendments Act. I expect to see something similar with RLUIPA.

At the other end of the continuum, where you are more concerned about protecting your private property from economic damage caused by the "negative externality" of an intensive activity next door, there is not much you can do to stop RLUIPA. The chances of a church cropping up next door, protected by RLUIPA, are slim. If there are legitimate public safety concerns that are the basis for denying the activity and that can be properly documented, there is a good chance that the activity can be stopped. RLUIPA generally does not protect activities that are related, but not central or essential, to the religious practice, such as schools and stores.

I guess one is left with a question: After the Fair Housing Amendments Act and RLUIPA, what will be next?

Chapter 3

Ten Keys to Getting Want You Want with Zoning

For those of you who are reading this book straight through, rather than jumping in at one place or another, this seems to be a good place to stop and summarize some of the lessons learned thus far, and integrate those lessons with some of what will come later. This may not be the most definitive list of what you need to do to get the most out of zoning, but it should help you organize your thoughts on what has come before and put into perspective what will come later.

1. Don't expect zoning to do more than it is capable of doing. Many other factors, including the market and the availability of infrastructure, are stronger determinants of land development.

2. Understand that zoning, as a local regulatory technique, is part of a much larger system of federal, state, and local regulation. Your challenge is to orchestrate numerous simultaneous permits and approvals at these three levels (and sometimes more, i.e., regional) of government to get what you want.

3. There are usually several different ways to address any one zoning problem, not one solution alone. You need to consider

alternative strategies and determine which one to play first and which one to play next, or which to play in concert.

4. Read the regulations from front to back and understand how they work together. The silver bullet may be found in some unusual part of the regulations, such as a table or appendix.

5. When it comes to zoning regulation the definitions rule. A small change, sometimes no more than one word, may create great value for you or irrevocably damage your property interests.

6. Modest, even innocuous, changes to a zoning ordinance can reap enormous benefits for you. A slight modification in a density formula or a permitted use may turn an ordinary profit into lottery-like winnings.

7. State and federal laws may override local zoning regulations, for better or worse. Understand how the state and federal laws interact with local zoning regulations.

8. Be ever vigilant as to what is going on with surrounding properties. Get local regulations amended to make sure that you get direct, personal notice before any changes that might affect your value can be made on any nearby properties. Consider private covenants and restrictions as a way to provide even more protection than public regulation.

9. Be diligent in the preparation for local proceedings because they may be the only chance you get to make your case. Use all of the local resources available to help you, and make friends in high places.

10. Develop strategies at the outset for administrative proceedings, litigation, and potential resolution of that litigation so that you know exactly what to do at what time to maximize the potential for success. To the extent you can, identify all eventualities, and develop risk and reward assessments for one approach versus another.

Chapter 4

A Short Course in the Law

 new house needs a good foundation. You need to know the basics of law to develop winning strategies.

Why Know the Law?

I'm a lawyer. Trust me; I'm not going to bore you. You need to know the basics of land use law so that you will be able to understand my strategies and create your own variations. You will also be able to impress your friends at parties with little tidbits such as, "Hey, I just read some really cool enabling legislation. How about you?"

Okay, it's not all that exciting, but it is important. It's about vocabulary. Behaviorists say that we really can't remember anything that happened to us before we were verbal. We need language to think and perceive. There is a myth that the Inuit have hundreds of words for snow. Not true, but they do have maybe three dozen. You and I can perceive or describe only a few types of snow, but because the Inuit have a vocabulary, they can see, understand, and communicate about more types of snow than you or I. I learned a little more about how this shapes our ability to perceive when I was consulting in Palm Beach County, Florida, and discovered that there are several kinds of palm trees. In the morning of the first day of my visit, before I learned their names and came to appreciate the differences, I saw only one kind of tree. By the end of the day, I saw five or six.

I promise you that by the end of this chapter, you will see the world differently. You will see the landscape of local land use law as I do—rich and varied, with lots of great opportunities to do new things with your properties.

"I Know It's Here Somewhere"— How Do You Find the Law?

"Look, let me tell you what the law requires. . . ." This is the way too many conversations with local officials begin. To understand what you can and cannot do, you need to know the law. To manage the lawyers you retain, you need to know the law. To be an active participant in your own land use matters, you need to know the law. To make money with your real estate and protect yourself, you need to know the law.

The Four Bases

There are fundamentally four bases, or sources, of the law: common law, constitutional law, statutory law, and administrative law. In one way or another, all law can be seen to come from only these four places.

1. Judge-Made Law, the Common Law

This one is talked about most often but in many respects turns out to be secondary to the other bases or sources of law in the land use business. This is the law found in judicial decisions. When someone says, "Did you hear the way the U.S. Supreme Court decided another takings case? Now those liberals on the County Council won't be able to tell us we must set aside open space," he is talking about judge-made or common law—the law of cases.

Case law is rich and inherently interesting. The cases start with a story line. The facts of a land use case often remind us of our situations. The application of the law to those facts results in a ruling, a holding that often creates a precedent: It tells us what the result should be in similar cases. We often focus on these cases because there are real people involved, we see the land, there are winners and losers, and there is the precedent that can be used against us or for us.

But hold it. Where do these cases come from? How did they get up to the appeals courts, and how were they decided with such publicity that they show up in the law reporters or newspapers?

The fact is that a large portion of these cases are mutants. They are weird and wonderful, but they are of little help to us in our day-to-day problems. Why? First, normal, rational people don't litigate if they can avoid it. It's expensive, and it's sometimes a crapshoot. I've had cases I would have bet the farm that we would win, and we've lost. And I've counseled clients that they would almost certainly lose, and we won. I've given up predicting outcomes. Of course, some outcomes are entirely predictable, but when both sides think they can win, they often find themselves in the kind of protracted litigation that results in the decisions you read about.

Second, even when one or both parties think they are likely to lose, they litigate to a final appellate decision. Sometimes they are driven by a strategy of intimidation or of trying to wear down the other side, to outspend them like a poker player doubling a bet on a bluff. Sometimes the parties have hidden agendas, or not-so-hidden agendas, on a policy issue. Many cases are engineered to create favorable publicity and a precedent for one policy position or another, so the participants battle to the end, trying to bludgeon each other into submission like two gladiators bound at the wrists. It's an ugly and unproductive business.

Finally, these cases, as land use cases, turn on the particular aspects not only of the property, but also of state and local law. A New Jersey Supreme Court case may suggest what the law should be in Oklahoma, but it is not precedent. Even a U.S. Supreme Court decision may be the "law of the land," but if it arises from a unique set of facts and has bubbled to the top as a result of the interplay of local and state law, the precedent may not be all that forceful or useful.

Most people, even lawyers, get much of what they know about case law from the press, and the press is inept at reporting these cases. A reporter from a national newspaper called me the day of a famous U.S. Supreme Court decision to ask my opinion. I was in a meeting and hadn't read it, so I declined. I asked if she had talked to others, and she said she had. She told me what they said about the decision. I asked if the "experts" she had talked with had read the decision, and she said they had not. That story appeared on the front page the next day with quotes from the experts, and it was wrong in many respects. The day after that, the same newspaper ran an editorial that was also off the mark. The misinformation begat misinformation, and the decision quickly evolved into kind of a legal myth. Don't believe the reports of a case you read in the press. If you really care, read the decision itself, and then say nothing for six months or a year until you have read all of the later court decisions applying the decision.

On the other hand, it must be said that the mythical perceptions of these cases have the force of reality. People cite them in hearings and wave them in the faces of opponents. They can be persuasive and carry the day at the administrative level. We need to recognize that and act accordingly. In the end, however, mythical interpretations don't win lawsuits.

In short, judge-made law, the common law, is important because it may create binding precedents and because people like to talk about cases and what they mean, but to command the field, you need to know how to use the other bases.

2. Constitutional Law

Here's a cocktail party piece of trivia for you: How many constitutions do we have in this country? Most people will say 1 or 2, but the answer is 51, one U.S. Constitution, usually with a capital C, and 50 state constitutions.

Constitutions are our basic template of governance. They are the contract between the government and the governed. They establish rights and protections, they give power, and they limit what governments can do. In the business of land use law, they are important.

Surprisingly, what is constitutional under the U.S. Constitution may not be constitutional under a state constitution. It is constitutional under the U.S. Constitution to limit the definition of families in a local zoning ordinance to persons related by blood, marriage, and adoption, and up to some small number of unrelated persons, but that same definition is unconstitutional in half a dozen states under their state constitutions. Therefore, in those states, the typical definition of family is not legal. Some state constitutions provide more protection for property rights than the U.S. Constitution. Some state constitutions have been interpreted to allow local governments to require that developers provide affordable housing.

Make sure you understand what both your state constitution and the U.S. Constitution provide—you may have some advantages you didn't realize.

Here are a few constitutional principles you need to know in order to have a powerful vocabulary.

Due Process

Due process comes in two flavors, procedural and substantive. Stick with me here. This is actually more interesting than it sounds coming out of the box, and it is the cause of more problems in zoning disputes than anything else.

Procedural due process is about how your rights to a fair proceeding are protected. You have a right to notice. The government needs to tell you what it is doing that may affect your rights. This can take a number of forms. Sometimes there's a letter to you. Sometimes the property is posted with a sign. Sometimes there's one of those fine-print newspaper advertisements. Sometimes there's only an agenda posted on the wall in the town hall. But one way or another, you have to have some notice when important rights are at stake.

You can shift some of the burden to the government by using the "sunshine" laws, "open meeting" laws, or "freedom of information" laws, all of which are different names for the same thing. These state laws (and there's a federal equivalent) allow you not only to ask for copies of all kinds of documents, but also to ask for notice of meetings and new items that are placed in the file. Consider filing a request for notice of meetings. Today, you can even get them by e-mail. Regrettably, some notices show up in the mail after the meeting is over, so simply asking for them in advance is not a guaranteed way to protect yourself. Vigilance is essential, which may mean stopping by the municipal offices and, yes, reading those fine-print advertisements.

Procedural due process means that you have a right to be heard. That right may be only the right to send a letter or to ask a question through the chairperson of a board, but you have a right to be heard.

You have the right to know and to confront all evidence. No one has the right to sneak something into the record without your having the ability to know that it's in there, although you may need to ask the government staff to see the file and look through it yourself.

People who are involved in your proceeding are not allowed to "get to" the decision makers without your knowing it. Your neighbor, for example, might telephone a commission member before the hearing and tell that person about how you run your business. That's evidence, and it must be in the record and in the public domain in some way, whether through a letter or through oral testimony at a hearing. If the commissioner allows your neighbor to provide such evidence outside of the hearing or record and doesn't disclose it to you, you have a right to have that proceeding reversed or reopened, assuming that you find out about it.

Don't make this mistake yourself, because you can be hurt as well. If you buttonhole your friend who is a member of the board or the commission at the golf club, and bend his ear with all kinds of factual information about an upcoming hearing—like the traffic problems you have seen at the nearby intersection—you put your own opposition position at risk. The wise board or commission member will have to "cleanse" himself of this tainted view—we call it an "ex parte" communication because it takes place outside of the hearing—by announcing your conversation during the hearing. That's very embarrassing. And it will be worse for you if it is not disclosed on the record but is discovered later.

But don't think that you or your friends are muzzled. In most states, you can express your feelings without their being considered evidence. You can tell the planning board chairperson that you think the new drive-through restaurant is not a good idea. That's not evidentiary—that's just an opinion. You can take out an ad in the paper and put signs on your property for or against proposals. The First Amendment right to freedom of expression allows you that.

I tell my clients to think of the ethical "light of day" test: How would you feel if the peers you respect heard of your communication in the "light of day"? If you feel uncomfortable, the communication is probably illegal as a matter of due process. Err on the side of keeping all these communications on the record.

Not only do you have the right to confront the evidence, but you also have the right to rebut it. In some types of proceedings you have more rights than in others, but at the least you have the right to put something in the record in response. To claim this right, you generally must assert it during the proceeding. If the opposition puts some factually incorrect testimony into the record or makes a claim that you want to contest, don't let the hearing close without offering your position. If necessary, stand up and interrupt the process. If you are shut off by the board, at least speak to your claim that you have been prevented from speaking: "Madame Chair, I respectfully object to your closing this hearing without allowing me time for rebuttal. Billy Bob's claims are unfounded, and I want to explain why. I have additional testimony and evidence." Now you have a record showing the violation of your right to due process.

What happens if, after the hearing is over and the vote has been taken, you find out that Billy Bob had a secret meeting with the chair before the hearing? A letter to the board demanding that the decision be set aside and the hearing be reopened might work in some states. At least it puts the issue squarely before the decision makers. Make sure that your information is verifiable—you don't want a slander or libel claim.

And if that doesn't work, raising the issue on appeal is still permitted even though you didn't first note it at the hearing, because, of course, how could you—you didn't know about it at that time.

Procedural due process problems arise after a hearing is closed and before the vote. A developer client once sent a helpful note to the commission after the hearing closed (without my knowledge, I should say) explaining that he would make a small change in the piping in the street as was suggested in the hearing. The chair received the letter the night of the vote, but told the commission that he would not consider it because the hearing was closed. The commission voted and approved the development. The neighbors sued and won, forcing the 400-unit project back for another round of rehearings. Why? Because the judge said that the chairman who read the letter, but didn't read it into the record or share it with the others, might have been influenced by it. This is an ex parte evidence due process problem. Now I tell my clients to forget about trying to be helpful and not to talk to anyone between the close of the hearing and the vote.

Procedural due process also requires that the decision makers be unbiased and objective. This is contrary to human nature. We are all biased and subjective in some way. Land use decisions often require subjective judgments—is the proposed development "harmonious" with the neighborhood, will it be "consistent with the character" of the community, is it too big or too small? In small towns, everyone knows everyone else, for better or worse. It's more typical than not to have someone from your church or your club or a distant relative on a board or commission that is making a land use decision.

What we look for is a disqualifying personal or financial interest. If the applicant's mother is on the board or commission, she can't vote. The president of the "Save a Swamp Today Society" also can't vote if the society has entered an appearance in a proceeding and has taken a position. These people—the mother and the swamp saver—have a personal interest in the outcome.

Someone who has a financial interest shouldn't be making decisions either. The 40 percent owner of an excavating company cannot sit on a board that is deciding whether to grant that company a permit to remove sand and gravel—she would receive a financial benefit from the outcome. I had a case in a town of just 1,200 people where the court disqualified a real estate broker from voting because the proposed project might create marketable properties and he might get a commission from the sales. That's pretty far out.

Many cases of personal and financial interest are too close to call. What should happen? First, any public official who has voting power and thinks that he or she may have such an interest should reveal it as soon as possible—to the chairperson and to the government's chief executive officer, chief elected official, and lawyer, if need be. Let them decide. Then, if the interest is so remote that it doesn't look like it really taints the process, decision makers can "cleanse" themselves by describing the apparent personal or financial interest and then stating that they will consider the evidence and decide in an unbiased and objective matter.

When in doubt, the official should step down—"recuse" himself, we say—and get out of the room until the hearing is over. I suggest getting out of the room because I have seen too many officials in this situation get caught up in the moment and cause problems when they try to participate in the meeting.

Finally, procedural due process requires that the decision be based on the evidence. The best way to ensure this is done is to have findings of fact and findings of law. The staff or board can draft them after the hearing is over, or the participants can submit their own draft versions first.

A finding of fact is just that. For example: "The project consists of 372 residential units on 512 acres." "The traffic at Main and Elm will increase by 27 percent during the peak hour, and the level of service [delay] will be reduced from B to C."

Findings of law are also as you would expect: "The proposed 5,200-square-foot video arcade is not a permitted use in the Business 2 Zone."

Sometimes, it's not possible to tell what kind of finding a particular decision is, but that doesn't matter: "The proposed shopping center will cause unacceptable congestion at the interstate ramp." What is important in terms of procedural due process is that the findings be made and that they be as specific as possible. In many jurisdictions, it is not acceptable to say: "The petition is denied because the proposal will be contrary to the public safety." This is too general.

See? Pretty interesting stuff, wouldn't you say? This is why this area of the law is so much fun.

Now, let's talk about substantive due process. Not everyone would agree with me, but I think this may be the most important constitutional principle in terms of the end result. While procedural due process is by far the predominant principle when it comes to absolute numbers of cases, court reversals, and general turbulence, substantive due process is what is at the heart of local regulation and decision making.

By *substantive due process* we mean that government regulation must be reasonably related to a permissible purpose of government and that governmental decisions must be made in furtherance of those permissible objectives. That's a mouthful, even from a lawyer. So let's break it down.

First, government can do only what we agreed it could do under the constitutions and, as we'll see soon, under the state enabling legislation. Suppose a local regulation says that no signs of any type may be displayed from a residence. You tape an 8½- by 11-inch sheet of paper inside your front window that reads: "Stop the war." The zoning enforcement officer issues a cease and desist order directing you to remove the sign. Does the regulation violate your substantive due process rights? Yes, it does. Why? The First Amendment to the U.S. Constitution protects your right to freedom of expression. This political speech is "pure" speech and is the most protected form of speech. You have no other reasonable opportunities to express your opposition to the war. The government never had the power to regulate this type of speech to begin with, except maybe the time, place, and manner of it, and therefore the regulation is not reasonably related to a permissible governmental objective.

Shifting to another illustration, suppose the government does have the legal authority to preserve open space for parks and state law allows local government to impose impact fees on developers to buy open space. You apply for a 10-lot subdivision to build 10 cottage homes for the elderly. The local regulation says that the village council may impose reasonable fees. The council assesses you $30,000 per lot for open space acquisition. Legal or not? Probably not. Although some fee is permissible, the fee assessed is not reasonably related to carrying out the government's objectives. There is no evidence to support the idea that one or two elderly people per unit would somehow create such a large need for open space preservation, and certainly $30,000 per home, unrelated to the home's size, expected occupancy, and value, is unreasonable.

You can use the substantive due process stick to your advantage to beat back regulations that go too far. If you're on the other side and are promoting more stringent regulation and more exactions from developers and landowners, you want to have all the support you can to justify the government's authority in the first place and then to support the requirements on a case-by-case basis.

Equal Protection

Everyone in the land-use process has a right to the equal protection of the law. Most recently, a question about this protection made its way to the U.S. Supreme Court in a case where a woman who had sued the local government over flooding was treated differently from others in an unrelated matter regarding a water hookup. The village delayed the hookup, and she claimed that this was vindictive action by the government that violated her right to equal treatment. The Supreme Court said that her claim was good enough to stay in court, and the parties were sent back to try the case.

In most land-use regulation, however, the name of the game is to treat different properties differently. That's zoning, isn't it? One area is for commercial, and one area is for residential. Like properties may indeed be treated differently. This does not violate equal protection.

Usually it is enough that there is a rational or reasonable relationship for the different treatment. A ridge top may be an area where trees cannot be completely removed or rooflines are not allowed to project above a certain elevation. Zoning may require houses in flood plains to be elevated. Buildings near airport approaches may be restricted in height.

When there is a suspect classification involved in a case, such as race or religion, or a fundamental right, such as freedom of speech, the government must come up with something more than a rational or reasonable relationship in order to discriminate. The government must show a compelling governmental interest. Prohibiting demonstrations close to abortion clinic entrances in order to avoid violence is an example of a compelling need. The First Amendment right to free expression takes a back seat to the more important need to protect the public's safety. Age is not a suspect classification, so age-restricted housing is permissible without showing a compelling need.

There's table pounding during hearings over equal protection, but it seldom comes into play.

Takings

The perceived loss of property rights in the age of greater governmental regulation has focused public attention on the takings clause in the Fifth Amendment to the U.S. Constitution and analogous state constitutional provisions. The Fifth Amendment says that the government cannot take private property for public use without paying just compensation. There are two types of regulatory takings. One is a physical invasion taking, such as when the government widens the street in front or your house or dams up water and floods your property without acquiring an interest in your property first. This physical invasion regulatory taking is to be distinguished from condemnation or eminent domain, two terms for the same thing, when the government takes your property but pays you for it. Regulatory takings are sometimes called inverse condemnation because they are like the regular condemnation or eminent domain turned on its head—the government takes but doesn't pay, at least until you sue and win.

The physical invasion regulatory taking is easy to recognize and easy for the property owner to win. If the government invades private property and converts it to public use, it will almost always have to pay.

For the property owner, the physical invasion taking is most likely to come up in a few rare cases. Local authorities allow a downstream owner to dam her property to control flooding, and as a result of her doing so, your property is flooded on a regular basis. As a condition of your zoning approval for a new store, you are required to provide a picnic area along a scenic overlook at the back of your property for the public's use. The Department of Public Works lays a drainage pipe from the street across the corner of your lot to connect with a nearby stream. The local airport runway is extended to your property line, and not only are you prohibited from building anything in the flight path, but the noise from the flights overhead makes your property practically unusable.

These cases are easy for the property owner to win. It is usually enough to show the invasion. There is no balancing of interests.

The nonphysical invasion regulatory taking is where the action is. Assume a 10-lot subdivision where the developer is required to set aside 2 lots for open space and dedicate those lots to the village. This is not a physical invasion of private property like the picnic table illustration because in this case the developer deeds the property to the village as a condition of approval. Two marketable lots are lost. The government's action has caused the developer to give the village one-fifth of the value. Has the government taken the property for a public use without compensation? Certainly there has not been any compensation, and the property is to be owned and used by the public.

In most states, this is not a taking and the loss in value is not compensable. The courts use a three-part test—that is, they consider three basic questions—with this type of noninvasive partial taking case. First, what is the loss in value? Here it is 20 percent of the total value. For a taking to be compensable, courts have often held that essentially all of the value must be lost. There are some cases where there has been over 90 percent loss in value, and the court still has not found a taking. Furthermore, loss in value alone is often not enough.

Second, what did the property owner have in mind when she bought, and what investment did she reasonably make in furtherance of those plans? The shorthand phrase for this is "investment-backed expectations." Assuming that the 20 percent land dedication was in place when she bought, the value of the land would have been for 8 lots, not 10, so she would not have overpaid for it.

If the law went into effect after she bought and after she had installed a road, water, sewers, storm drainage, and the like for 10 lots, she might have a claim that her reasonable investment-backed expectations were for 10 lots. She might even claim a vested right for 10 lots, in which case the court might hold that this new land dedication requirement did not apply to her subdivision. She would not receive compensation for the taking, but she would get the 10 lots upon invalidation of the government's requirement as to her project.

The third part of the test requires a balancing of the private burden against the public benefit. The loss of two good lots is a substantial one for the developer, but perhaps the public need for open space outweighs the private loss, especially since the eight new families moving into the area have created some of that need.

This third part of the test is highly subjective. Only in extreme cases does the result seem apparent. Think of a prohibition on photofinishing or chemical storage in an industrial park that is discovered to be over the source of the town well. The private burden is small, and the public risk is large. At the other extreme is a regulation limiting the height and placement of coastal homes to protect the views from properties behind them—a large private loss and little or no public benefit.

The First Amendment—Expression and Religion

The First Amendment has several provisions, but freedom of speech and religion are the two that are of interest in zoning and land use. The First Amendment may be the most important and powerful of the amendments. In the land-use arena, there are often stark conflicts between individual constitutional protections and protecting the public's interest.

Freedom of expression includes all of the sign issues plus, believe it or not, adult entertainment.

Government can regulate the time, place, and manner of signs by showing only a rational or reasonable relationship to a government interest, such as aesthetics. However, government cannot regulate the content of signs unless there is a compelling objective. Off-premises commercial signs ("Mary's Muffler Shop—Two Short

Miles Ahead!") get the least protection; on-premises commercial signs ("Home of Mike's Burgers") get a little more protection; and pure speech signs expressing political and religious views ("Jesus Saves" "Vote for Joe" "End the Stupid Tax Hikes") get the most protection.

Believe it or not—and I have made a thorough study of this, even to the extent of visiting many of the establishments at issue (only in the interest of scholarship, of course)—strip clubs are protected by our Constitution. The reason is that the live performance is a form of expression. Proponents have successfully argued in some cases that sexual arousal is part of the message. It's hard not to smile in wonderment at how lawyers can wage their wars in these cases with a straight face. The courts have put a tight net around adult uses, including book and video stores, and have even upheld restrictions requiring pasties and G-strings as not violating the First Amendment. Think of this speech as way out at the fringe of protection, far beyond the off-premises commercial signs and close to being entirely unprotected, just as obscene and inciting speech ("fighting words") is unprotected. Government can severely restrain adult entertainment uses, but it may not be able to outlaw them entirely.

The religion part of the First Amendment has two clauses: free exercise and establishment. People have a right to freely exercise their religious beliefs. Churches use this clause to argue for their right to locate on a site. If you hold prayer meetings at home with a few people and the zoning enforcement officer issues a cease and desist order, this is the clause you will invoke.

The establishment clause prohibits a government from favoring one religion over another. Do you remember the recent dust-up in Alabama over the judge who fought to keep a stone tablet with the Ten Commandments in the courthouse? That was an establishment clause case. When your village allows a church to place a nativity scene in the public park, it is likely to lose a challenge under this clause.

Congress's enactment of the Religious Land Use and Institutionalized Persons Act seems to give religious groups a leg up. There have been over 100 challenges to the law, and whether it will survive constitutional attack is yet to be seen. If you have a case involving a religious use, start asking about RLUIPA (remember, "ree-loop-a"). The effect of RLUIPA provides us with a nice bridge to the third of the four bases of the law.

3. Statutory Law

In the zoning game, the statutes rule. Most zoning power comes to us by statute at the state level.

Think back to fourth-grade civics. The federal government is a federation of the states with limited powers conferred by the states. That's the theory, at least.

The fundamental power of governance arises in the states. It is called the police power, but it goes way beyond the people with badges. The police power is so fundamental (like the old, "because I'm your mother, that's why") that it is often not even expressed in the state constitutions. It is the power to protect and promote the public's health, safety, and general welfare.

This fundamental power is at the core of all land-use regulations. Please reread that phrase and commit it to memory: the power to protect and promote the public's health, safety, and general welfare. You will use it again and again.

Now we can link back to substantive due process. Whatever the government is regulating has to fit within the four corners of this mantra. If it doesn't come from the police power, the government can't do it.

Here's something that makes even my law students shake their heads and local commissioners groan when I say it, but it's true. Local governments have no power in their own right. No power. None.

How can that be? It is because local governments are creatures of the state. They get their authority to regulate from the police power life source. It is beamed down to the local governments by the home-rule authority that some towns or cities enjoy in the form of a local charter—a grant of power from the state. It's like giving your teenager the keys to the family car.

For local governments without a charter, the state grants them police power through the enabling statutes. All state zoning enabling statutes are descendants of a model law that the federal government promulgated 80 years ago. By now these enabling statutes have suffered from so much political wrangling that it is hard to find the shared lineage, but it is there. If you keep nothing else in front of you in terms of legal authority, make it the enabling statutes. You can find them online in most states. Be sure to get the newest amendments, called *slip laws*. Print the enabling statutes and read them. You will be surprised at how much you can learn. Many of the old salts think there is nothing new in there for them and have forgotten important provisions and surely missed the new ones. Your knowledge will be your power.

The statutes provide both procedural and substantive law. The procedures tell what you must submit and when. They say when the government must decide and how. They provide the process for legal challenges. Be very careful about procedure. You may have the best case, bar none, on the merits, but you can lose everything if you or someone working for you makes a procedural misstep. File too early, file too late, file the wrong thing, fail to make a record, forget to object—it's a minefield out there. I was an expert witness in a case where a lawyer got sued for malpractice because the surveyor on the project put the wrong date for the hearing on the sign required to be posted on the property. While they were straightening out the notice problem, the zoning regulations were amended, cutting the number of lots in half. What a mess.

The substantive law in the statutes is about what can be regulated. Can the government dictate whether you have to have a pitched roof or you can have a flat one, can it require you to enclose your boat and trailer with a fence, will you have to pave your driveway, will it be your responsibility to provide a traffic signal off-site when you expand your factory? Many of these answers can be found in the enabling statute or the cases interpreting the statute.

4. Regulations—Administrative Law

Administrative regulations implement the statutes, common law, and constitutional law. They sound, and often are, so boring that we are tempted to and often do slide past them. Not a good idea. These laws are still laws, and the law is the law.

The U.S. Army Corps of Engineers has regulations to beat the band. The federal Environmental Protection Agency has even more. State governments and local governments have regulations. Be careful, though, when you talk about the local zoning regulations. These "regulations" are actually the equivalent of state statutes because of home rule and the enabling authority. True regulations do not usually require the formal adoption procedures used to enact zoning ordinances/regulations. In the end, the nomenclature matters not. Statutes and regulations both have the force of law.

The best land-use practitioners know these administrative regulations inside and out and play them like a Tennessee fiddler at a harvest-time hoedown. The zoning sniper—the person whose mission it is to knock off a proposal—can bring down big game with a legal slingshot if the regulations provide the right target. I saw a super-regional shopping mall project die from the delay caused by successful snipers who ran the hapless developer and its lawyers ragged. If you know these regulations inside and out, you won't make mistakes in the application process. If you want to cause heartache for an opponent, know the regulations, pick a good issue, raise it, and pursue it, and when that issue is resolved, pick another and pursue that. Applicants will be smart, when they sense this strategy, to demand that opponents bring out all objections once they start. This is not legally required, but it does have an impact on the decision makers who value fair play.

Congratulations and a Practice Pointer as a Reward

Congratulations! With your successful completion of this chapter, you have completed most of the work that law students cover in half a semester. I have spared you from reading the cases, but as I said early on, the cases are not all that instructive.

Because you have been diligent and attentive, I will now share with you one of the most powerful pointers I have: If you don't like the law the way it is, change it. You can do it. I do it all the time.

Changing the case law is a long, expensive, risky, and uncertain process, but I've done it by picking the issues carefully and lining up the right parties. I don't recommend it as a first step.

Changing the U.S. Constitution is beyond unlikely, and changing the state constitution is almost as difficult.

The federal and state statutes, however, are pretty much a work in progress, as near as I can tell. Without their inherent mutability, we would have to open new homeless shelters for lobbyists. A chapter or more could be set aside for examples. A few statutory changes are illustrative: a change to make six developmentally disabled people the equivalent of a family, no matter what the local definition;

federal override of local zoning to allow disabled persons to live together in group homes; relief from zoning restrictions for affordable housing; vesting of property rights upon filing of an application; protection for certain uses from later changes in regulations; and RLUIPA, mentioned earlier, giving religious organizations some new leverage in siting their facilities.

Local regulations (serving as local statutes) are subject to the same amendment process. With major developments, a new client will usually ask what the plan and local regulations allow. I tell the client to conceptualize the project first, to make it the best project possible. We say it must be profitable, marketable, and approvable. The developer takes care of the first two; we do the last. A really good concept sells itself, and smart communities will amend their plans and regulations to fit the project.

The same goes for government regulators and interest groups concerned with too much and poorly designed development. They can and do routinely seek to amend the local law.

Never take the law as a given. If it doesn't work for you, no matter what your agenda or objective, change it.

PART II

GETTING READY TO MAKE YOUR MOVE

Chapter 5

Know What You Have

Every successful campaign requires careful planning and preparation. In Vietnam, I used checklists to get my ship—a 38,000-ton, 655-foot-long tanker—underway. We would start two days in advance with lighting off the boilers for our steam plant. Can you imagine what would have happened if we hadn't planned for that? Today, we use checklists with dozens (yes, dozens) of pages just to identify what federal, state, and local permits may be required for a major project. In this chapter, we'll look at what you need to do to get ready for getting what you want.

My first land-planning professor, Professor Ted Bacon at the University of Massachusetts, told us in 1966 that planning involves three steps: What do you have, what do you want, and how do you get it? I have never heard a more powerful formulation, and, if you apply it, it will help you be successful.

What Do You Have?

Determining what you have requires that you take two different perspectives, one of them looking inward at your own property, and the other looking outward at the surrounding area and the larger community. We look at the latter in Chapters 8 and 9.

The Project and Your Land

You must assess your objectives. What do you want to achieve? Over what time frame? What are you prepared to give up? What is your staying power? How much time, energy, and money are you willing to expend? Let's save that discussion for the next chapter, "Know What You Want," and look first at your property and the context within which it is located. What exactly did you buy or what are you buying?

Astonishingly, many people, even experienced real estate investors, are unfamiliar with what they own or what they are buying. They know the lot area, the building size, and the use and dimensional requirements of zoning, but they know little or nothing about what is in the title. Just as Professor Bacon taught me as a college sophomore, before you can proceed with planning for the development of your property, you need to know what you have, and knowing what you have requires understanding exactly what rights and obligations you acquired with your piece of dirt.

What property rights you own are determined, in the first instance, by the deed or other grant by which you have received ownership of your property. If you don't have a title search already, you may want to get one. If the title search you have is an old one, you probably need to have it updated. Any of the several title insurance companies can undertake a title search for you for a reasonable cost, about $150 to $250 for a single-family detached lot.

The title search will tell you what you purchased. It will describe not only the location of the property, but its land area, its dimensions, and the abutting owners. Importantly, a title search will also tell you what rights and responsibilities were conveyed along with your title. (Well, at least it will tell you what rights and responsibilities there are of record, or recorded in the land records where your deed is recorded as a matter of title. As we shall soon see, other rights and responsibilities may be evident on the face of the land, but not necessarily in the record title.)

In reviewing the title report, you might want to look for rights in the form of an easement across other property, such as a driveway or an underground easement for laying water, sewer, and other utility lines. An easement may protect a scenic view across another person's property. I once represented a bank president who was buying a lot and building a house on Nantucket that was one lot removed from the waterfront. He wanted to protect his view of the water, so we negotiated an airspace easement over the intervening waterfront lot owned by the same seller, preserving the bank president's view of the water and restricting the owner of the abutting lot from placing any structure on that portion of the property where it would block the view. This type of easement is not necessarily one on the ground, but might start several feet above the ground along the sight line.

In 1968, while working as a planner straight out of undergraduate school, I helped create the same type of airspace restriction, much like a long, small box suspended in the air, from the Route 16 bridge in Wellesley, Massachusetts, down along the Charles River, so that the views to the river enjoyed by pedestrians while they crossed the bridge would be preserved.

If you have a fabulous view from the portion of the property you want to develop, you might consider putting restrictions on the balance of the property that you sell off, so that you can preserve that view. This doesn't leave the other property undevelopable, it only limits the portion of the site that the new owner can use.

Similar restrictions were often imposed 25 years ago, when we were more concerned about solar access. However, with the economics of photovoltaics now justifying the solar generation of electricity, the time has come to consider routinely imposing airspace easements over properties, so that the roof of one house can look out over the yard of another house to get access to the sun. Without such an airspace easement, your neighbor can allow her trees to grow up and block your access to the sun, preventing you from using that free resource.

Not all incidents or matters of title are necessarily for your benefit. There may be restrictions or encumbrances on your property that create burdens for you. One example is an obligation to maintain portions of your parcel as undeveloped open space. I once had a case where the top executive of a national company had purchased a beautiful waterfront home in a resort town. In his yard, between the house and the shoreline, was an elaborate sunken garden with expensive masonry. And in his deed, unbeknownst to him, was an easement of access across his property for the benefit of the neighbor on the other side, who did not have direct access to the water. He retained me to straighten it out. I told him he basically had two choices: He could either attempt to relocate the easement to another portion of his property or relocate the garden. The answer was obvious: I should attempt to get the easement relocated, which I did after some negotiation with the neighbor.

Another case involved a large international company that had a 400,000-acre corporate headquarters. The company had gone through several mergers and acquisitions and eventually was broken up, like many big outfits in the early 1980s. In the process, I was called on to retenant the corporate headquarters, which was empty as a result of the break-up.

Many years before, as a concession in the process of getting the original zoning approval for the corporate headquarters, the company had agreed to a restriction on the property limiting its use to one corporate tenant. The rationale was that a single corporate tenant would manage the property better than multiple tenants, so that there would be less potential for an adverse impact on the surrounding residential neighborhood—an area of mansion homes.

Had this been merely a zoning restriction, we might have dealt with it by simply petitioning the zoning authority for an amendment to the original approval. The neighbors, however, were much too sophisticated to allow that simple restriction without some additional protection for their individual properties. They exacted from the developer a "negative easement" running from the corporate headquarters site to many of the single-family lots in the neighborhood, giving each of the owners of those individual homes the right to enforce the one-corporate-user restriction on the headquarters property.

Like many things in life, it seemed like a good idea at the time.

We managed to get the zoning restriction changed after some wrangling and a concession that the corporate headquarters would be limited to four companies and no more. Deliveries were restricted to certain hours during the day. All that worked well in terms of making the building economic. What about the neighbors?

Each of them was a beneficiary of the easement, and each and every one of them had the power to prevent the conversion of the building to multiple tenants. The company had little bargaining power, except for the fact that it was increasingly obvious to all concerned that something had to be done, because the building would never again be used for a single corporate tenant, and without the conversion it would stay empty—which was not good for the neighborhood.

In the end, the company paid each of the neighbors a substantial sum of money to release the one-corporate-user restriction.

A surprising amount of information can be gained by simply walking the property and the neighborhood. Many restrictions on the use of the property are evident from visual inspection. For a visual inspection to be useful, you must view not only the property to be purchased but also the substantial area around it.

The surrounding uses and their relationship to the subject property may not always be obvious.

We had one case, some years ago, where we represented a man who had purchased a property abutting a small general aviation airport, which he didn't realize was there because the airport was screened from the house by a wooded area. There was also a substantial change in elevation, which placed his house well below the end of the runway. The little airfield was seldom used on weekdays, so there was no evidence of small planes coming and going.

The first weekend after he and his family moved into the house, our client discovered the presence of the airport when small planes flew low over his roof, which was right on the centerline of the runway. He wanted out of the deal. He wanted the sellers to take the house back.

Making the case even more challenging was the fact that the client was a highly qualified commercial pilot who had thoroughly researched the properties he had considered purchasing. The sellers (are you ready for this?) were an order of nuns. The pilot had asked them whether the house was quiet, and he reported that they had said it was. Our objective in the case was to get the sale rescinded on the grounds of misrepresentation as to the condition of the property. We sued the nuns and the real estate broker. What a mess, and what an unfortunate situation for all concerned.

In the end, the case was settled after some litigation. The pilot sold the house with full disclosure of the presence of the abutting airport, and the order of nuns retained the purchase price. An insurance company for the brokers helped in bringing the parties to terms. The town, interestingly, was one of only a handful in the state that did not have zoning, so public regulation provided no protection. The new buyer converted the house to offices, which was entirely compatible with the airport next door and was easy to do in the absence of zoning regulations. Title insurance would not have provided any protection in this situation. The general aviation airport was virtually invisible during weekdays, when there was no activity, and could not be seen, at least readily, from the surrounding road system.

Among the lessons learned here are that a buyer cannot be too careful in inspecting the property and its environs, and sellers should never make any representations about the condition of their property. It is almost always best to work through a broker or third party, to insulate the sellers from any claims that they may have intentionally or inadvertently misrepresented the condition of the property.

A land surveyor does the same work on your physical property that the title searcher does on your legal property in the land records. A surveyor can locate the boundary of your property as described in the deed. It often happens that a neighbor unknowingly (or maybe knowingly) has been using your property as if it were his own, such as by erecting a fence on your land, mowing a lawn in an area that you own on the far side of your stone wall, or extending his garden into your property.

Did you know that you can actually lose the title to your property if you let your neighbor use it as his own for a long period of time? This is called *adverse possession*, and the length of time varies from state to state. It is usually in the range of 15 to 20 years. If your neighbor uses your property in a way that is "open, notorious, conspicuous and adverse"—and throw in some more similar legal words—then he may get title to your property if he brings a claim in court for adverse possession. By the way, this does not hold where government property is concerned—you cannot get an interest in government property by using it in the same way that your neighbor might use your property. The government cannot lose property by adverse possession. Nor can some other owners, like the railroads. On the other hand, the general public can get an easement over your property by "prescription," which results from the public's use of your property over time, such as a path across your backyard used by children going to and from school.

You know those barricades that you sometimes see on the plazas in front of big buildings downtown? They are usually there one day each year, with a note on them indicating that the plaza is private property. The purpose of these barricades is to cut off the public's access for a short period of time. The public's use of the privately owned plaza is interrupted so that it is not continuous for the period of time required to create public prescriptive rights over the private property.

You can cut off this running of the period of time for adverse possession in most states by giving your neighbor some type of notice that you dispute the claim. This is definitely an area where you need to consult with your legal counsel promptly, because any delay might prove damaging.

If a few feet might make a big difference to you, it is worth the time and effort to have a surveyor actually survey the boundaries of your property, and to consider staking or monumenting the boundaries. The surveyor will also identify on the plan the location of any man-made structures, particularly stone walls and fences, and any prominent features such as a rock outcropping or large-diameter tree, and indicate whether they are actually on your boundaries. If stone walls and fences don't coincide with your boundaries, but you assume that they do, you may be losing value to the neighbor who is using or, worse, adversely possessing your property. The surveyor will also report the presence of any indications of activity that may suggest use by others, such as a cart way or path, a wellhead, or any area of excavation.

There are many "common-law" rights and responsibilities running with your property in addition to what you might find in your legal title and what you might find by a careful personal and professional inspection of your property and environs. The common law is judge-made law, much of it ancient law and custom dating back to Roman or early English times.

You do not have the right, for example, to flood your downstream neighbor's property, but you may have reasonable flowage rights across her land. If you think it is hard to draw the line between reasonable flowage rights and the prohibition on flooding a neighbor's property, you're right. You may find these rights and responsibilities if they are in your deed and in that title report, and your surveyor should be able to tell you what they are, but they are potentially there, nevertheless, deriving from a body of law and custom dating back hundreds and even thousands of years.

One of the more important common-law or ancient-law restrictions on the use of property is the "public trust." The public trust dates back to the Code of Justinian. It is the right of the public to use land in common. Its effect is seen most dramatically in coastal areas, where in most states the public has the right to fish and take fowl and to pass and repass below the high-tide line. In other words, you can spend $5 million on the oceanfront home of your dreams, only to share "your" beach with a gang of beer-guzzling fishermen.

Many of the more important cases arising out of the conflict between the protection of private rights and public trust rights have arisen where the government has prohibited a private property owner from dredging or filling waterfront property. Believe it or not, because of the public trust, you generally do not have the right to place a protective seawall below the mean high-water mark to save your property from being washed out to sea by erosion.

In one recent instance, a private property owner waited too long to apply for a seawall. The state gave his neighbors permits for seawalls at an elevation higher than the mean high-water mark, and therefore out of the public trust area. Their properties were saved from erosion. The property of the owner who delayed in applying for a seawall was rapidly washed out to sea, and by the time his application was processed, the proposed location of the seawall was at an elevation lower than mean high water and therefore subject to the public trust. The state denied his seawall permit.

He lost his property (literally), and he sued the state, claiming that it had "taken" his property by denying the seawall. The court denied his taking claim on the theory that he did not have the right to place a seawall in the public trust area.

What have we learned? First, take a hard look at your property and the area around it. Get aerial photographs, some of which are available free on the Internet. Get government topographic maps and walk the entire area around your property, making sure that you have seen all corners of your land and that you know its boundaries and how the surrounding land is being used. Get a new title search, and read it in detail. Ask your lawyer or the title insurance company to explain anything you do not understand. Get an owner's title insurance policy, not just one insuring your lender. Hire a good surveyor and go over the survey results in detail, and consider staking or monumenting boundaries—at the least, any that you don't know. Ask the surveyor to help you identify any potential interests in your property that are not of record. Check with local government officials as to any zoning requirements that have already been imposed on your property and on surrounding properties. You might even look at the titles and the zoning records for surrounding properties to see what rights and responsibilities have been imposed on those lands. Have your lawyer brief you on the common law, and how it affects your land and what you want to do with it. The most powerful statement you could make at this first stage is: "I don't understand that. Explain that to me." Don't be afraid to ask, because what you don't know, I guarantee will hurt you.

Remember what Professor Bacon told us—the first step in the planning process is to know what you have.

Know What You Want

Be Realistic and Protect Yourself against Risk

Developers, even sophisticated ones, sometimes make the mistake of having unreasonable expectations. They may think that they can get 200 lots from a parcel that more realistically can carry only about half of that number. They may hope for an expeditious permitting process, without realizing or accepting the possibility that a strong-willed neighborhood group could tie the project up in litigation for years. Mistakes as to what the market is are often made at the outset, and many developments do not have a sufficient "cushion" built into them to make the development feasible at a lower density or with a more protracted approval and development schedule.

No one has to be a developer or real estate investor, except maybe Donald Trump, who somehow seems genetically disposed to the profession (and also to reality television, which is not far removed from real estate investing). There are other ways to make and lose money, and the alternative is always simply not to do the deal or not to undertake the project, but to invest in something else.

The important point is to make the effort to sit down and write out realistic objectives for your real estate investment and zoning campaign. What is your "home run" scenario for your property?

That is, if your assessment of the market is correct, and you can get what you want in terms of zoning, what is your project?

Now, suppose that your market prediction is off just a little bit, and suppose that you run into trouble with your local zoning authorities and need to reduce the density of your project, say by lowering the total number of residential units proposed from 200 to 150—would buying this land at the price offered make economic sense, or would you be, as we say in the trade, "under water?"

Take your several scenarios of the market, including your expectations of how the market will change over time and the problems you might run into with zoning, and lay them out with various timelines. What happens if your "normal" approval process, instead of being six months, becomes three years, because an opposition group appeals, first to the court, and from there on up to the appellate courts? Have you budgeted for the cost of this litigation? Have you calculated the carrying costs—taxes, insurance, and a mortgage—for such a protracted period?

Some of the most successful developers with whom I've worked have a way to shift elements of this risk back to the property owner. Obviously, if you already own the property, you can't shift the risk back to the seller. Regardless of who owns the property at the time you start the development process, you're unlikely to be able to shift any of the additional cost of the delay and reductions in development potential to the purchaser, because the market is what the market is—you can't sell your lots, for example, for 10 percent more than what the market says they should sell for just because it cost you 10 percent more to get them approved.

If you are dealing with a seller, however, you may be able to get her to take some of the risk. If you structure the deal so that you're going to pay X dollars if you get 100 units and Y dollars for each additional unit, then if, during the process of zoning approval, you are forced to reduce the density by 50 units from the 200 you expected, you have effectively passed that risk back to the seller. I say "effectively" because economically it is more complicated than that. The fixed soft costs—such as engineering, design, and legal costs—won't vary much between 100 and 200 units, and the fixed hard costs, such as road and utility construction, also will vary little.

How well this attempt to shift the risk back to the seller works depends on the deal itself. Sellers may require an increasing return per unit ($Y for units 101 to 150, $Y + 2 for units 151 to 175, and $Y + 3 for units 175 to 200) because of the increased risk that you will get bogged down in a zoning process where you were perhaps too aggressive in trying to achieve a dense project. Worse yet, from the seller's perspective, your aggressive zoning campaign creates the real risk that the property will be "tainted" for some time. If the local zoning authority is left with bad feelings caused by a developer who mismanages a zoning campaign, the seller may pay the price by having a property that is unmarketable for a period or that can be developed only for a substantially less profitable use.

Just as the risk of reduced density can be passed back to the seller, you may be able to pass back the risk of delay. Our typical development deal, where we have a zoning contingency, is to give a modest down payment and make additional payments over the period of the zoning campaign. The down payment and the additional payments may or may not "go hard." "Going hard" means that the payments become the property of the seller, regardless of whether the project goes forward. The developer won't get her money back if she can't get the zoning approvals when the payments have gone hard. Developers try to avoid having their payments go hard, and even if they can't prevent that from being part of the deal, they will attempt to make the payments applicable to the purchase price; that is, the payments are applied to reduce the purchase price that is finally due.

To the extent that the seller is getting no increase in the purchase price during the time of the zoning campaign, the seller is financing the carrying costs of the project. When a seller does that, he is likely to require a higher price for the property, given the risk of delay.

Contract provisions for a project involving a modest zoning campaign generally include a down payment and some fixed period of time to complete the zoning, such as one year. That time period for closing would be automatically extended by whatever period of time it takes to defend a zoning approval in court or to prosecute the appeal of the denial. Because these time frames are unknowable, they are often stated in terms of some additional time (say, one year) as may be necessary to prosecute the appeal through the court of the highest competent jurisdiction, but not to exceed some fixed period of time (say, three years) unless the purchaser pays an additional price (say $Z/month hard, and not against the purchase price, for up to 36 additional months).

Assessing the Possibilities

When you purchased your property, you carefully reviewed the zoning regulations, and you have a complete command of them, right? Let me tell you, it is unrealistic to expect that you should have a complete command of the zoning regulations. Even those of us who do zoning for a living every day are often confused by complex local regulations. It is astounding how jumbled many of these regulations are. They have become a crazy quilt, stitched with hundreds of amendments over many years. Important substantive provisions are buried deep in the corner of some table or appendix or definition. We generally read the zoning regulations from front to back twice before we even attempt to interpret or apply them. Even then, one can't always give a definitive answer as to what is permitted and what is prohibited.

There is a doctrine in the law that says that a board or agency that is interpreting its own regulations is given broad discretion in interpreting them. Consequently, we will often ask the board itself, or its staff, what a particular regulation means. Sometimes we will research the history of that agency's decision making to find a pattern or practice of interpretation.

Even then, reasonable and appropriate expectations for objectives in your zoning campaign may not be obvious. You also may want to look at surrounding communities to see what their zoning regulations require.

We had one case where a property owner who had 5 acres wanted to establish a riding academy, but the local regulations required a minimum of 15 acres. When we looked at the eight to ten surrounding towns and other towns of similar size in the region, we found that most of them had no minimum lot area for a riding academy. In the couple of towns that had a minimum, it was only 3 to 5 acres. We took that information back to the local zoning a board, and it amended the ordinance to allow the academy on 5 acres.

Sometimes a standard is found in industry practice. Retail developers and operators have their own standards, such as for parking ratios; these are generally consistent with local practice, but that may vary. A typical parking ratio for a shopping center might be 5 parking spaces per 1,000 square feet of retail sales area. The parking ratio might be lower, say 1 or 2 spaces per 1,000 square feet, for merchandise storage, loading and unloading, and food preparation areas. The ratios are also likely to be lower for the office areas within retail establishments. These numbers are generally accepted in the industry, and, surprisingly, they sometimes require more parking spaces than the local government might require. For example, some retailers want 6 spaces per 1,000 square feet, whereas the local requirement might be 4.0 or 4.5 or 5.0 spaces per 1,000 square feet.

It is important when establishing your own zoning objectives that you understand the industry standard and what the market requires.

The market may dictate your objectives. For example, your local zoning regulations may require two parking spaces per dwelling unit for an apartment or condominium project. However, a market analysis in your area may reveal that it is important to have an additional parking area for guests, and perhaps even another area for recreational vehicles and boats. We also have seen some interest in the marketplace in self-storage on site in connection with higher-density residential developments.

Finally, you will want to consider the widely accepted standards published by credible authorities, such as the American Planning Association and the Urban Land Institute. These organizations, and many others, have published development standards, which are useful for informing real estate investors, developers, and regulators.

All right, you know what you have and what you want. Now the fun really starts: learning how you can get what you want.

Chapter 7

Know How to Get It

If you have been with me from the beginning, I'll bet you could almost write this chapter by yourself.

The key to knowing how to get what you want from zoning is to always think in terms of orchestrating a variety of approaches and to identify all of the alternatives for getting the result you seek. You also must establish a sequence by which you will proceed so that you maximize the number of alternative approaches and the opportunities to succeed.

Let us take a look at this process, with illustrations for various types of properties. This should be more interesting and informative than identifying the techniques and sequencing in a vacuum.

Splish-Splash, My Girls Want an Above-Ground Pool

You are a homeowner who has purchased a wonderful ranch house built in the 1960s. The zoning has since been changed, and your quarter-acre lot (10,000 square feet) is now nonconforming because the zoning is been increased to require half-acre lots (20,000 square feet).

While your front-yard setback and your side-yard setback conform to the newer regulations, the rear-yard setback of 30 feet is encroached upon by an elevated wooden deck that predates the change in zoning.

Your house is nonconforming as to dimension because of the encroachment of the preexisting deck into the new larger rear-yard setback. That is not a problem for you, however, because under the regulations you have the right to continue to maintain this deck forever. You just cannot expand it further into the rear yard.

You do have another problem, however. For the last two summers, your two daughters have been asking you to get an above-ground pool, as one of their friends down the street has one. It seems like a good idea to you, and you have already picked out one that is on sale at the nearby pool and spa company. You get plans from the store, and you go see the zoning enforcement officer to determine what permits and approvals you'll need for the pool.

Guess what? Under the terms of the local zoning regulations, the above-ground pool is a structure, and structures cannot be placed in the rear yard. The only structures allowed in the rear yard are fences along the property line, if they are not higher than 6 feet, and one accessory building, such as a garden shed, with a floor area not greater than 48 square feet. In-ground pools are not subject to the full 30-foot rear-yard setback, but may be placed within 10 feet of the rear property line. However, an in-ground pool is way beyond your budget, and you don't contemplate keeping the pool after your daughters have graduated from high school.

You know you have some options. You can tell your daughters that the zoning doesn't allow the pool they want, so they can't have one. That's not the right answer.

Think back to the prior chapters and what we have learned thus far. Take a piece of paper now, and outline all of your strategies for solving this problem. Close the book as you do this, and then come back and pick up where you left off. I think you'll find that you already have a good command of orchestrating a variety of alternatives to use in solving this problem.

It's nice to have you back. It wasn't that hard, was it?

First, that's exactly right: You want to read the zoning regulations from front to back (twice!) to determine whether it is only the half-acre zone that has the requirement on the siting of above-ground pools or whether one of the other residential districts has a lesser requirement. If there is more lenient regulation elsewhere, you may have a good argument for getting the zoning for this district amended. You also want to ask the city, town, or county clerk, whoever is the repository of historical records, to get out the zoning regulations as they were at the time your house was built. Look at the quarter-acre zone as it existed when your house was built. Maybe above-ground pools were allowed. Maybe they were not even addressed as structures at that time. Maybe the rear-yard setback was only 10 feet for above-ground structures not attached to the house. This information will be important to you in one of your later strategies.

Next, you will take a look at surrounding counties and towns to see what they have in their half-acre residential districts, and perhaps in their quarter-acre residential districts, which is effectively where you are because you have a nonconforming use. If some or most of those other jurisdictions would allow the above-ground pool in your physical situation, this may be very important to you in convincing the local zoning board to give you permission to have your pool.

It could be useful to know how many other homes constructed on quarter-acre lots already have pools. It will make a good point as part of a fairness argument if you can show that many others already have pools that predate the change to half-acre zoning or that many lots are still in the quarter-acre zone and are able to install above-ground pools.

You will probably then want to look at some of the standards published by authoritative sources, such as the American Planning Association. What do their model regulations provide with regard to above-ground pools in rear yards?

Armed with this information, you will meet with the town planner, the building official, or the zoning enforcement officer—whoever is the immediate contact—and that person's full-time staff with regard to local land-use regulation. You will ask about the possibility of seeking some relief from the restrictions so that you can get that above-ground pool for your daughters.

Perhaps the first thing you should do in this type of situation is to seek a modest amendment to the zoning ordinance. You might petition for an amendment that would allow above-ground pools in the rear yard as of right on the same basis as in-ground pools up to within 10 feet of the rear property line. "As of right" means that no type of approval or hearing is required, other than simply applying for and having the building official issue you the building permit.

Instead of making this as of right, you might request an amendment to make it by conditional use, special permit, or special use permit. These are all the same type of regulatory approval; they just go by different names in different states. They are somewhat discretionary approvals; they are almost as of right, but they require a site-specific review and usually a public hearing.

A typical special permit use is a church, funeral home, or dentist's office in a residential district. These types of uses might work on some parcels, but could be a problem on others, so the local government needs a site-specific review.

An above-ground pool hardly rises to the potential impact that a church, funeral home, or dentist's office would have in a residential neighborhood, but you're certain that you can get your neighbors to come out with you and support approval of your above-ground pool. Your strategy in suggesting a special use for above-ground pools in the rear yard in the half-acre residential zone is that such an amendment will be more acceptable politically and will be judged to be a minor modification to the regulations. An as-of-right amendment for above-ground pools would be likely to be seen as a more significant change to the regulations (because it would be!), and you don't need it to get what you want in the end. All you want is the right to apply for something that you are quite certain will be approved in your particular situation.

What else could you do? While it may be a straightforward strategy to amend the ordinance to allow an above-ground pool as a special use in the half-acre district, you could take a simpler route and amend the definition of "structure" to exclude above-ground pools. In-ground pools, you will recall, are already exempt from the rear-yard setback. Above-ground pools are not presently exempt, presumably because they have a greater visual and physical impact in the rear yards. Still, you might apply for that change in the definition, maybe with a limitation on the overall height, the footprint (the length times the width), or the bulk or volume (the length times the width times the height).

I don't know of any regulations that limit the bulk of above-ground pools—I just made that up. But that's exactly what you should do if it helps you get your approval by limiting what you are asking for. It occurs to me with this hypothetical that an above-ground pool up to a certain bulk or volume could be allowed if the existing house had not used up all of the potential volume based on the setbacks and height. Very few houses, except the McMansions that have sprung up on small lots in the older suburbs, ever use up all of the bulk. It seems a fitting argument to say: "Why shouldn't I be able to make use of the potential bulk on my property that I haven't used with my house? I would rather have it in the form of an above-ground pool than as an addition or a second floor or dormer on my existing, older home." Makes sense to me, and it is hard to argue with.

How about another type of amendment? You could propose a separate rear-yard setback just for above-ground pools so that they could be allowed in a portion of the setback, perhaps with a greater setback than for an in-ground pool but enough so that you still have sufficient area behind your house to construct the pool.

You might try drafting all of these modest amendments and discussing them with staff. In the next couple of chapters, we'll talk about how to short-circuit this process by building relationships.

Another approach is to amend the regulations to carve out your class of property for special relief, given your nonconforming status. For example, an above-ground pool could be allowed as of right or as a special use in the half-acre residential district in the rear-yard setback to within 10 feet of the rear property line, if the residence was constructed prior to 1970. The effect of this approach is to point out that these older homes are disadvantaged under the newer regulations. It also has the effect of limiting the number of locations in which above-ground pools can be placed in the rear yard. Presumably, the owners of newer homes built under the current zoning have the opportunity to design their yards with sufficient space to provide for above-ground pools. Owners of older homes constructed under the prior zoning have no similar opportunity, because the dimensional requirements under the change in zone have been imposed on them.

How Else Can You Get What You Want, besides Amending the Zoning Regulations?

A *variance* might allow you to put the above-ground pool within your rear-yard setback. The city or county council or zoning board or planning board, depending on the state you're in, administers the zoning regulations. A zoning board of appeals or board of adjustment or board of zoning appeals (all the same thing; the name just varies) can grant variances from the zoning regulations.

The zoning board of appeals (ZBA) in most states generally has three functions. It may have the authority to grant some special permits. It also reviews appeals of zoning enforcement decisions, such as when the zoning enforcement officer (ZEO) says that the back steps you want to build are a structure that would illegally encroach into a side yard, but you believe otherwise, so you appeal the ZEO's interpretation to the ZBA. Sometimes a ZEO will issue a cease and desist order when the ZEO believes that the zoning regulations have been violated. There have been several widely reported cases of ZEOs enforcing zoning regulations on dutiful and loving fathers who have built tree houses for their children without benefit of a zoning permit or building permit. A property owner may appeal the cease and desist order to the ZBA, and if the owner doesn't win there, she can appeal to the courts.

The third role that the ZBA plays is to grant variances from the zoning regulations. The power to grant variances was added to the proposed standard state zoning enabling act in the 1920s to prevent takings of private property by overregulation and to provide a degree of flexibility that the drafters felt was necessary to make zoning politically acceptable and workable.

A variance can be granted when there is a "practical difficulty and unnecessary hardship" unique to the property. Variances are granted from dimensional, bulk, and density requirements. For example, if something unique to the property, such as a rock outcrop, prevents a detached garage from being reasonably located on the lot and a feasible location would encroach into the required side yard only a few feet, then it is likely that the ZBA would reasonably find that there was a practical difficulty and unnecessary hardship resulting from the unique physical condition on that lot.

Use variances are disfavored in the law, and many states and local governments do not allow them or severely restrict their use. It is fair to say that use variances are overturned in court more often than dimensional variances. A use variance might be a gas station in a residential neighborhood. A gas station might not be permitted under the zoning regulations in a residential zone, but a property owner might claim a practical difficulty or unnecessary hardship given existing development in the area, particularly non-conforming uses. There have been a few rare cases where courts have upheld use variances.

I'll tell you something about the odds in variance cases so that you'll have a better idea of when and where to put your money down. The late Professor Donald Hagman, in his treatise on land-use law, said that about 90 percent of variances are granted illegally. That's my experience as well. You would think that there would be lots of litigation over variances and many successful plaintiffs who have challenged the issuance of variances granted to their neighbors.

There are not many variance cases, at least relative to the number of variances that ZBAs grant. Why? Because most people simply don't care, and they think it is fair that their neighbors should be granted the variances they receive. The ZBAs grant variances when they think it is equitable to do so.

Here is an example I use with my students. Mrs. McGilicuddy is in her late sixties and recently widowed. She was forced to get a driver's license, but she couldn't drive her late husband's old stick-shift pickup truck. She bought a nice old Buick, and she has been parking it outside in the driveway near the cherry tree. The car is being stained by the cherries dropping off the tree, so she gets a local carpenter to design a carport on the side of her house by the kitchen door, and she goes to the building official for a building permit, only to discover that the carport will encroach three feet into her side yard.

She could leave the car out. She could build her carport in the back of her lot like some of her neighbors, but that would cost considerably more. The building official suggests that she apply for a variance, and she does so. The variance is granted without any real discussion. The couple who live next door come to the ZBA hearing with her and say that they support the variance for the carport.

Is there a practical difficulty and unnecessary hardship because of a unique physical circumstance affecting that lot alone? No way. Give me a shot at widow McGilicuddy and she won't have her variance much longer. But no one is going to appeal it because no one cares. The members of the ZBA often see their job as one of being equitable and helping people where the neighbors either don't care or actively support the variance.

Sometimes, the best, and perhaps even the only, place to start is with a variance, even though you know that there is no way you can honestly meet the "practical difficulty and unnecessary hardship" test. I once had a case involving an old strip shopping center (we now call these "open" centers, because it sounds better). The owners wanted to expand the center and put in a large building products and home improvement center (that limits it to two possible retailers, doesn't it?) where a defunct small department store had been operating. There were literally six different ways in which the zoning regulations prohibited this expansion of the nonconforming center, but the town wanted to see the center redeveloped, and the planning staff was completely supportive.

We applied for six different variances—lot coverage, parking, landscaping, and whatever else. The ZBA unanimously granted all six variances after a straight-faced finding of "practical difficulty and unnecessary hardship" based on the fact that this was an older, existing center that was physically, functionally, and economically obsolete in its current layout. No one appealed the variances, and the center was rebuilt.

I was once waiting my turn at a ZBA hearing when the lawyer before me got up and said: "Now, I know this is really not a basis for hardship, but as you know, my client was tragically burned and is presently in the hospital, where he has written this letter asking for a variance from the dimensional requirements. He wants to subdivide his large lot into two lots, which would otherwise be illegal, except that with a variance, he can do it. He needs the money, and it really will have no adverse impact on the neighborhood." The ZBA approved it with little discussion.

And so it goes.

It's Just a 10-Lot Subdivision, You Know . . .

Let us switch to a commercial example of a zoning campaign, based on a common scenario.

You have been subdividing land in New County for the last 10 years, but the political climate is changing; the regulations seem to be more stringent, and elected officials are increasingly demanding of developers. New issues are now coming up in many residential land subdivision proceedings, including the preservation of open space, environmental protection, and affordable housing. It is becoming increasingly difficult to make good money with residential subdivisions.

Farmer Burns has decided to sell off 15 acres of his property in order to finance the college education of the family's oldest son. You have an option on the property, and, having read *The Complete Guide to Zoning*, you structure the deal with a small down payment, applicable to the purchase price, six months to get through the subdivision process, and a modest additional payment for six more months if you get bogged down in permitting. Your deal includes an extension beyond that for monthly payments to carry you through up to three years of litigation. You are proud of your record of having never litigated a land subdivision case, and you have had only one denial in the last 10 years. You were able to walk away from that option with little economic damage. The planning board likes you, and you have a good relationship with the board members, but the political climate is changing, and there is increasing "grandstanding" by newer members of the elected board.

Your plan is to do 10 lots of one acre each (these will be full-acre lots of 43,560 square feet). Some land will be lost because of inefficient lot design, and the balance of the remaining five acres will be taken up by a cul-de-sac road right-of-way with sidewalks on each side.

You take a sketch plan of the subdivision and stop by the county planning office to see Millie Barnes, the county planner. You have your usual pleasant chat with her, but then she begins to get more serious, and she tells you: "The planning board has asked me to update our open space regulations to require subdivisions smaller than 25 lots to include open space. If you get your application in quickly, you will have a vested right to proceed without setting aside open space, but I don't think the planning board will be too pleased with that. On top of that, with interest rates so low these last few years and high demand for new homes, housing prices have run up considerably. New County also has become a desirable place for retirees. That segment of our population is increasing rapidly, just as we knew it would with the World War II baby boomers aging into retirement. They need affordable housing. There has been lots of discussion during the last few meetings about affordable housing, and they're even looking to small projects like yours to help on the affordable and senior housing front. Finally, as if that was not enough, we seem to be looking around for good models of so-called green subdivisions—subdivisions that minimize the impact on the landscape and show some evidence of being designed for sustainable development."

You're beginning to think that maybe you should have stayed in the farm implement business.

Rather than proceed with the sketch plan that you showed Millie, you decide to go back and sit down with your engineer and land surveyor to see if there might not be some modest changes that could be made to the plan that would preserve its profitability, and at the same time play to some of these emerging issues. Your engineer and land surveyor recently attended a multistate regional conference of the American Planning Association, and they seem to be full of good ideas.

"Suppose we try to work all of these objectives into our 10-lot subdivision to see if we cannot preserve all of the profitability, and maybe even improve on it," says your engineer. That doesn't seem possible to you, but you agree to start reworking the plan.

First, you discuss how you might be able to get some additional land for open space. "Although New County has not adopted cluster regulations, many other places have, and we could use cluster regulations to reduce the size of each of the 10 lots just a little and put the extra land in open space," explains your land surveyor. He goes on to describe how a neighboring county allows clustering in one-acre subdivisions to reduce one-acre lots to 30,000 square feet, with the difference in area (13,560 square feet) being set aside as open space. There is public water to your site, but you will have on-site septic systems. The soils are good, and your engineer assures you that you can get individual septic systems on each of the lots even with only 30,000 square feet.

It looks like it may work physically, but what about the market? You discuss some recent subdivisions in the abutting county, and you agree that they have done well and that sales prices have been consistent with those in conventional subdivisions with slightly larger lots.

"Well, how do we even get the planning board to buy into this concept?" you ask. You then discuss the strategy for doing this, and you decide to propose a modest amendment to the zoning and subdivision regulations allowing such cluster developments on parcels of (you guessed it) 15 acres or more. What has worked in the abutting county will almost certainly work in New County. You cut and paste a proposed draft of the amendments and set it aside for further discussion with Millie at your next meeting. When it comes time to have the regulations amended, you will ask the county planner in the abutting county to send a letter to New County officials, explaining how well the cluster provisions have worked.

Before leaving the subject of clustering entirely, you and your consultants work out some of the savings that might result from clustering. The frontage requirement in the one-acre zone is 175 feet, which means that you will have about 900 feet of roadway, with five lots on each side facing each other. You may be able to get down to 125 feet of required frontage per lot with the cluster lots, which will reduce the road length to about 625 feet, saving about 275 feet of road. At over $200 a lineal foot, you will save between $60,000 and $80,000 in road construction costs. The county will save money in road maintenance. This cluster idea is beginning to look better and better and worth the additional time it will take to get the planning board to adopt the necessary regulations and approve New County's first smaller cluster subdivision.

"I can't imagine there is much that we can do to make this a green subdivision," you say, more to yourself than to your engineer and surveyor. "Oh, no," your surveyor responds. "Not only is this something that you can do, but I think we can save you some real money on the development costs. You can look good to the planning board and have a more profitable development." He goes on to explain that planners and environmentalists are increasingly getting away from the traditional catch basin and culvert system of disposing of storm water, piping it from the streets and discharging it directly to streams, in favor of "leak-offs" and "sheet-flow" systems. These systems essentially keep the storm water on the ground and have it filter through the grass and be absorbed in shallow depressions along the side of the street. In this way, the pollutants in the water are removed; they either are trapped in the top few inches of soil or evaporate into the air, rather than being discharged into a stream and carried away to cause pollution offsite.

In addition, your engineer explains, developers are beginning to use so-called rain gardens in connection with runoff from roof drains. Rather than take that runoff and discharge it to spreaders on the ground and into catch basins and culverts, roof drains are being discharged into small gardens, maybe eight feet square, alongside the house, where plantings are maintained. The plants get the water, and the water seeps through the soil and is returned to the earth, rather than running off into the streams. This results in fewer contaminants coming off the site and natural groundwater recharge, all of which are characteristic of green subdivisions.

"And the best part is that with this 10-lot subdivision, if I redesigned it in this way, I can save you at least $5,000 per lot, or $50,000 for the subdivision, by eliminating the catch basins and culverts," says your engineer. Now, you're no longer slumping in your chair, but sitting up straight and thinking about how that savings of $50,000 would go right to your bottom line, along with the savings in road costs. Maybe, saving open space and doing a green subdivision will be a good thing. When you go to the planning board for the amendments and approvals for this new green subdivision, however, you won't mention the cost savings for the developer. Rather, you will express an interest in protecting the environment and point out that home purchasers today have a greater interest in being part of the environmental movement.

Your engineer and surveyor then explain that making these changes is going to take some work—not principally on the design side, because there's enough literature out there on how to do it, but in making additional changes to the zoning and subdivision regulations. Back in their offices, they have sample regulations from a national environmental organization, and they think that those models will work in New County.

But affordable and elderly housing? How is that ever going to compute? This is an "exurban" county, just beyond the suburban fringe, where even one-acre subdivision lots are considered somewhat dense. You're never going to do an apartment or townhouse project in New County, and with on-site septic disposal, it wouldn't be physically possible anyway, unless you got into an expensive permitting and construction effort for a small sewage treatment facility to service a higher density.

"Our homes are going to be expensive, make no mistake about it. We can't downsize them, and we can't do more of them. The elderly don't want big, expensive homes, and we can't make them small enough or cheap enough to do what Millie says the planning board wants. We're stuck," you tell the engineer and surveyor in frustration. The three of you stare at each other for a while, and then you remember last month's state home builders' newsletter, sitting there on the corner of your conference table, which has a discussion about the increasing use of "accessory apartments" to provide inexpensive, smaller units for young singles, young couples, empty-nesters, and seniors.

You reach over, slide the newsletter in front of you, and open it to the story about accessory apartments. Your engineer and surveyor have read about them, but largely in the context of converting large older homes that are too big for today's families. The usual idea is that you carve out a small portion of an older house and create a separate one-bedroom or studio apartment inside the envelope of the building, usually for an elderly person who wants a rental unit. Sometimes these apartments are designed the other way around, so that the elderly person can stay on in his large home and rent a small unit for additional income, and perhaps receive some day-to-day support from the young person or couple renting it.

But you're in the business of building new houses in new subdivisions. Is there a fit, and how can you use this knowledge of current land development techniques to leverage your way into not only an approval, but a more profitable project? Successful real state investors and developers work hard and spend a considerable amount of time keeping up with the latest trends. They don't want their local planning boards and planning officials to get out ahead of them when it comes to the emerging issues of public policy concerning land use and development. Just as a successful lobbyist serves as a conduit for information to legislative decision makers, the successful real estate investor and developer brings to local government the latest land-use information and techniques.

Reading further in the article, you discover that some communities have begun to allow accessory apartments, defined as one-bedroom or studio units of not more than 600 square feet in new homes, on a limited basis, such as not more than 20 percent of the homes in a new development. "Hey, this is good; I think there is something we can do here," you say to your consultants. You pick up a set of stock plans that you will be using for the four or five different model homes that you may build in the subdivision, and you take a closer look at the "El Conquistador" model, which has a Spanish motif and is about 2,800 square feet, including a "bonus room" over the two-car garage.

"How about we convert the bonus room and a portion of the hallway and the walk-in closet from the master bedroom suite into a 650-square-foot, one-bedroom accessory apartment, which can have a separate entrance behind the garage and a small deck for the tenant's use? The plumbing will line up with the master bedroom suite, and we can put a full bath right behind the master bedroom bath and a kitchenette adjacent to that. It's a nice space, and it is separated from the rest of the house." Your consultants agree, and it is decided that 2 of the 10 homes in the subdivision, both of them "El Conquistador" models, will have accessory apartments. You do some quick figuring, and you conclude that the bonus room space can be converted to the accessory apartment at an additional cost of only about $20 a foot, or $12,000, and that an affordable monthly rent of $500 will provide a net positive cash flow to the homeowner. It's a good deal all around.

The next day, you drop by Millie's office and lay out the revised sketch plan of a cluster subdivision, discuss the redesign of the storm water system, show her some examples of rain gardens, and tell her about the concept of doing 20 percent of the new homes with accessory apartments designed for singles, couples, empty-nesters, and seniors. Millie is thrilled with every aspect of your proposal and says that she is going to discuss the matter directly, and privately, with the chair of the planning board to make sure that the board will be as enthusiastic as she is. She suggests that you meet informally with the board before you file any of the proposed amendments to the regulations or make your application, and she promises to put you at the head of the "new business" agenda at next week's meeting, once she has assurances, informally, from the chair of the planning board that all of this will be acceptable.

The heck with farm implement sales . . . this is a lot more fun and profitable.

There Is Still Room in the World for an American Toy Manufacturer

Your grandparents were in the toy business, making wonderfully handcrafted wooden toys in Brooklyn starting in the late 1800s. They kept on with the business, and your parents eventually took it over, and it went on to your generation. You're now reaching your seventieth birthday, and you're asking yourself, how can this company survive in the face of the tremendous pressure of imports in the toy industry, particularly from China?

You have managed to keep your small manufacturing facility with about 75 employees nonunion, but the plant is very expensive to rent, as land prices in Brooklyn continue to rise and the neighborhood around you is being gentrified. Your lease is up in two years, and you're becoming increasingly afraid that this could be the end of a three-generation business, simply because you will have no place to manufacture at a price that allows you to compete with imports. Your line of exquisitely detailed model wooden trains and the complex layouts that collectors have made from your train sets are respected worldwide. How are you going to keep this business going?

You need about 100,000 square feet of manufacturing space, including a place to store inventory and raw materials, a shipping room, and office space. You are hopeful that the business will not only survive but grow, at least modestly, so you want another potential 50,000 square feet of space for future operations. The space, in any event, must be inexpensive.

You start working with a national real estate broker, explaining your needs. The broker finds a great facility next to the rail yards in Raleigh, North Carolina. The old building, which used to be part of a metal-finishing operation for the manufacture of automobile engine manifolds, has been empty for more than a decade. The city of Raleigh's economic development department is eager to get a new owner and to provide new jobs. The state of North Carolina has a program to subsidize new manufacturing activities in the state. Labor costs are low, as are utility costs.

You fly to Raleigh and meet with the local broker. At that meeting, you talk about engaging local counsel to assist you. The broker identifies three law firms in the region that have the capability to handle the land-use and environmental matters for sites such as this.

Environmental matters? I mentioned that it was a metal-finishing plant. Bells and whistles go off when we say metal finishing, because it is virtually certain that with a 100-year-old facility like this one, there will be soil contamination from the solvents used in the manufacturing process. Indeed, this site is on a state list of contaminated properties for which there must be some remediation or cleanup. This type of development site is called a "brownfield" site, a reference to the color of tainted soil.

You have read plenty about contaminated sites. It has never been an issue for you at the Brooklyn factory, because you have done only woodworking. With the exception of the paint room, there isn't any part of the factory that might have contamination. Now you ask yourself, do you really want to get involved with a site that is on a list of contaminated properties, given all of the potential liability that might be involved?

The comedian Jonathan Winters, who was hospitalized at one point in his life for treatment of mental illness, was once asked how he felt about that. In response, he pointed out that he was one of the few people he knew who was certified sane. What we like about brownfield sites is that once you are done with the federal and state review and approval of the cleanup, you stand very little chance of any further liability.

You enter into an option agreement and confidentiality agreement with the existing owner allowing you to undertake investigations on the property, and you promise to keep the information confidential. A significant issue for the seller is that the contamination on the site might be more extensive than the state listing shows, and the seller does not want you as the potential purchaser to reveal anything new.

You engage an environmental consultant, who undertakes a Phase I survey, which is largely a visual survey of the property and a review of public records. The Phase I report documents the record of solvent contamination on the property. Your consultant undertakes a Phase II analysis and identifies an area of contamination that is limited to a room that contained a dip tank. The contamination appears to be only in the top several feet of soil, and the Phase II report suggests that excavating the top five feet of soil in an area of about 600 square feet will remove the worst of the contamination.

There is, however, evidence of other moderate contamination across most of the property, and the recommendations following the Phase II report suggest leaving that in place and resurfacing the parking lot areas with three inches of asphalt. There are no groundwater supplies in public use in the area, and there is no concern about groundwater contamination given the relatively low levels of solvents in the soil. The seller gives you permission to share the results of the Phase I and Phase II analyses with federal, state, and local officials.

After consultation with the local lawyers and meetings with state and local authorities, you are satisfied that a deal can be struck to limit the remediation given that the future use of the site will remain manufacturing. A much more expensive and complex cleanup would be required were the site to be converted to something with a greater chance of direct human contact, such as a residential project. In return for the agreement that you will not have to remove all of the contaminated soil, you agree to restrict the use of the property to manufacturing and not to penetrate the barrier placed over the contaminated soils. This restriction will be placed on the land records and will run with the land just like any other covenant and restriction.

Your consultant has put a price tag of about $300,000 on the remediation, not including the repaving of the parking lot, which has to be done anyway. You are justifiably somewhat concerned that other contamination might be discovered during your work on the site, so you have your lawyer begin negotiations with the seller for a hold harmless and indemnification agreement to protect you should more widespread contamination be discovered after you close.

You and your lawyer are both concerned that the seller will be "judgment-proof" because the seller is a corporation that has limited assets and is likely to be liquidated in the next several years, once it is rid of this real estate. You suggest that the deal include insurance for the additional potential environmental risk, and you begin discussions with the seller.

You also have talked with state and local economic development officials about "tax increment financing (TIF)" to help cover the cost of the environmental remediation. Under the TIF program, money for the environmental remediation will be advanced to you from state bond money, and then the state will be reimbursed for those funds by the municipality out of the additional tax revenues that come from your improved real estate. In other words, the future revenues from increased taxes pay for the current cost of getting rid of the environmental problem. What you care about, of course, is that the problem with the property you are going to buy is being fixed at no additional cost to you. More found money.

Would that the brownfield problems were all you had to cope with at this factory site. . . .

There are zoning issues—after all, this is a book about zoning.

The building, being just over 100 years old, is nonconforming in just about every respect. It has the 100,000 square feet, more or less, that you want, but there does not appear to be any opportunity to build a 50,000-square-foot expansion should your business succeed, as you hope it will, in this new location. You have no current plans for the expansion, and you certainly do not have the money to invest in creating plans for submission for a building permit. Regardless, even if you use one of the several techniques we previously discussed, from amending the regulations to getting a variance, your rights in that 50,000-square-foot expansion would not vest until you undertake "substantial construction in reliance on a validly issued building permit" (perhaps you recall those words from elsewhere in this book).

It's time to dig into your bag of tricks for yet another technique to solve your problem. This time it is the all-powerful "development agreement" that will lock you in for 25 years, or whatever period you negotiate, so that you will have the absolute right to make that 50,000-square-foot addition to your building.

Development agreements are bilateral contracts between the local government and a landowner. Most of zoning and the discretionary controls that are found in zoning, such as special permits and site plans, and the equitable processes of relief, such as variances, are unilateral, or one-sided. You apply for approval, and the government grants it, denies it, or grants it on certain conditions. There isn't any bargaining, at least in the formal sense (although there is quite a bit of horse trading behind the scenes and in subtle and not-so-subtle ways during hearings).

Development agreements put the bargaining right up front, and just about anything is fair game. I represented the developers of Kiawah Island after they bought it from the Kuwaitis when it was about half built out, with perhaps 3,000 of a potential 7,500 residential units already in place. A dispute arose between my client, the owner and developer of the balance of the land at Kiawah Island, and the administration of the local government. The administration had concerns about the plan for the rest of the island, although there was already an approved detailed master plan. To settle the dispute and lock in the balance of the development of Kiawah Island, we negotiated, as co-counsel with a local law firm and the developer's personal lawyer, a detailed development agreement in which the developers agreed to do certain things (like provide land for a town hall) and the government guaranteed the developer the right to finish the project essentially as it had planned.

From the developer's perspective, the development agreement is a vesting agreement by which the developer can be guaranteed the right to complete a project over a long period of time, without regard to changes in the local administration and without having to undertake any substantial construction. The "price" that the developer may pay for this long-term guaranteed right can take many forms.

You, as the potential factory purchaser and operator, should expect to guarantee something to the local government in return for the irrevocable right to expand your facility. It may be that you must agree to give preference to local residents in the hiring process. You might be required to undertake a job-training program. You might be required to locate any further plant expansion in Raleigh. The development agreement might provide for some additional payments to the city, in return for having the privilege of future expansion.

The development agreement is not a substitute for zoning, however, and you still need to get approval for the expansion under the existing regulations, either by amending those regulations or by having a variance granted. The development agreement should absolutely protect you from any future changes in the regulations, except those that are essential to protecting the public's health and safety. If, for example, you agreed to provide 200 parking spaces for the total factory build-out of about 150,000 square feet, regardless of what happened with parking ratios under the regulations, you would still never have to provide more parking than the amount specified in the development agreement.

A development agreement is the perfect solution for a large, complicated development like Kiawah Island. Such agreements are also just the thing with projects that have a long build-out, on the order of 30 years or more. Developers are appropriately reluctant to invest heavily in high-capacity infrastructure at the front end of a project if they don't know that the density at the back end will justify that initial investment. Development agreements can lock in that later density and in that way support large up-front expenditures. The development agreement would be just the thing for your factory, given the uncertainties in the future in the wooden toy business and your need to have the assured right to expand. If you're going to relocate to Raleigh and take on the site, you need to be sure you have the right to provide additional production capacity in that location without moving again.

So there we are—three quite different examples of how to get what you want with zoning, but all three have more in common than they have differences. The overarching themes include orchestrating a variety of approaches, sequencing your strategies so that you preserve fallback alternatives, and conscious bargaining to get what you want without making large changes that will affect many other properties in the community.

Create and Leverage Relationships

I tell my young lawyers—and I can imagine one of them in particular smiling as he reads this because he hears it from me often—that it is "all about relationships." That is, of course, an overstatement, but I have found in my long years in this business that building, maintaining, and then using good relationships is essential to our success.

If you're going to be in the land development and real estate investment business, you need to care about people, and that caring must be evidenced in your actions and your attitude. It is not something that you can simply wear on your sleeve; it must be part of the way you relate to people day to day.

Communication

It starts with communication. No stakeholder and no one with any responsibility wants to be left out. Have you told the right people in the right order about what you plan to do? Have you consulted with people who may know more than you do, and asked for their advice? Did you think to thank someone who helped you? When I meet with local officials and they are helpful to me, which they invariably are, I will frequently call them up later and send an e-mail or a handwritten note (I keep boxes of note cards in my office for just this purpose) to thank them for spending the time with me. I appreciate it, and they deserve the thanks. When I get done with a project, I often send thank-you notes and sometimes letters, which I copy to their bosses. Sometimes I draft the letters on behalf of my clients, and they send them. It gives me pleasure to extend this thanks to all concerned.

The point is that you need to communicate from the beginning, perhaps even before you buy the real estate or come up with a development idea. That communication needs to continue throughout the project. Even after you get everything you want with zoning, you need to follow up and maintain those relationships, just as you maintain your relationships with your family and friends.

One technique that is becoming practically essential for any of the larger zoning campaigns is the operation of a Web site as a communications device. We use project Web sites to put up pictures of the proposed project, to describe the community benefits, and to solicit input. We don't create chat rooms or other mechanisms by which people (including objectors) can exchange information, but there is an opportunity for people to send messages back. We collect those messages frequently, review them, and send replies. Sometimes the submissions indicate an interest in assisting as a consultant on the project (we get many of these). Numerous inquiries are from people who may want to buy or rent at the completed project. This provides an excellent database, available at the marketing stage.

Show You Care

Establishing, building, and maintaining relationships does not mean giving gifts. In fact, in today's climate, about the worst thing you can do is give a gift of any value to a government official. But there are gifts with no intrinsic value. They can be important. Did you see a good article in the newspaper about something that the chair of the planning board has an interest in, such as whether skateboard parks are a good thing for a town? Did you clip that article and send it to her with a note saying that you thought she might find it of interest?

If you see a newspaper story with a picture of someone who is important to you in this business of land development and real estate investment, you might consider asking the newspaper for a clean print of the photograph to give to the people in the picture. I also sometimes make a good copy of the article on nonyellowing paper and have the photograph and the article framed together.

Be careful of the rules regarding giving and receiving gifts, especially for public officials (where it is generally prohibited) and within certain corporations (where "nominal" gifts sometimes are acceptable, but more valuable gifts must receive preapproval from higher-ups). Anything of value received by public officials or employees is potentially forbidden, so consider the cost of anything prepared or given. A city manager was recently quoted in the newspaper as saying that his staff had paid back a developer during a meeting for coffee that the developer brought in. That will give you some idea of the degree of sensitivity to gift giving.

Most people are too modest to buy and frame a picture and an article about themselves (an exception is my beloved separated-at-birth brother and law partner, Alex MacDonald, who has many articles about his exploits, friendships, and great victories hanging on his office wall).

If you give someone a picture of himself (this reminds me of the story I read to my children about giving a mouse a cookie) that he can set out somewhere in his office, he will enjoy it. And when his visitors inquire about the picture, he'll say: "Oh, yes, that's a picture of me from the newspaper. My friend Dwight gave it to me as kind of a gag gift. It's kind of fun, don't you think?" I like giving gifts like this, because I know they are something that the recipient will continue to enjoy over and over again.

You don't have to give a gift to show your appreciation for someone. You can make a contribution to a charity that the person supports. You can volunteer to help her in her charitable or community-service activity. You can attend community events and show your support simply by being there. Community-spirited real estate investors and developers frequently give of their time and expertise by volunteering to be members of boards and commissions. Such participation provides an opportunity to get to know elected and appointed officials on a personal basis, without regard to a particular project or controversy. They get to know you as an individual, and this makes it a lot easier to communicate with them on a project later, because they will see you as an individual, not merely as a proponent.

Create a Database of Contacts

Just about every person I meet, just about everybody who writes to me, just about everybody I write to, and just about everybody who attends a conference that I attend or speak at gets a place of honor in my contacts file. For many entries, I have a note about where I met the person. If I have information about the person's spouse or children or hobbies, or something else of special interest, I will put that in there too, so the next time I have occasion to be in contact with this person, I will be reminded of something that is important to him.

I have over 6,000 contacts. When someone asks me if I know anyone in Denver, I can go into my contacts, search for "Denver," and come up with a long list of people from Denver that I have met or corresponded with. That list helps jog my memory about important aspects of the contact (she is a landscape architect; he mostly represents ski resorts; she was one of the historic preservationists who helped save SoDo).

I have a friend who is an in-house lawyer in a national corporation that develops facilities all over the country. She calls me every once in a while, asking for information about people in some location, and she always prefaces her question with: "I know you must know somebody [wherever], so I thought I would call."

Lyndon Johnson was known for keeping notebooks with the names of virtually everyone he met. Having these contacts helped him get what he wanted from politics.

You do not have to be someone who works across the country to use the system to build, maintain, and leverage your relationships. This is just as important in your hometown or county or state. My good friend Frank Schnidman, for example, puts everyone's birthday on his calendar. I know that even if one of my siblings just happens to forget my birthday, I will always get a card from Frank. You might do the same with some subset of your contacts.

You can maintain a holiday card list or list of anniversaries; maybe even including the day on which your important project was approved. On the first anniversary of that approval, you might write to the mayor and the planning director, thanking them again for their help.

There is no excuse today, with the powerful database systems available, not to keep contacts that will permit you to reach out for support for your projects.

Be Accessible

Some of my partners and peers roll their eyes at this suggestion, so you can take it or leave it. It gives me great comfort and helps the people I work with for me to be available 24/7. I answer my own phone most of the time at my office. I carry a cellular phone all the time, although usually only my assistant and my family have access to the number. My assistant passes on all calls coming into my office to me during the times when I'm away from the office, when she knows I'm not in meetings. I do not like to play telephone tag. It is inconvenient for people who are trying to reach me, and, more importantly, it is inconvenient for me to try to call them back. Also, more often than not, I shut my phone off when I am in a meeting. I do not want the person I'm with to feel that she should play second fiddle to some stranger coming in on my phone line.

If something is urgent, I will explain to the people in the meeting that I might have to take a call. Or I will have my assistant send a message to me on my wireless e-mail or a short text message to my pager, which is set on vibrate so that it doesn't disturb others in the meeting.

While I'm on the subject of respect and not having interruptions, let me say that I can often tell if somebody on the other end of the line is playing with his computer, reading a magazine, or eating a sandwich. I myself have been caught more than a couple of times trying to "multitask" (even computers can't actually multitask; they simply switch quickly from one task to another), and I now discipline myself to be isolated from all other distractions when I'm on a call. It makes the call go more quickly and is a sign of respect to the caller.

My pager, which I carry all the time, is tied into my voicemail at the office. I tell my clients and other people with whom I need to maintain contact, such as local officials, that they can call my office 24/7, and I will be notified of their call and will get back to them just as soon as I can. This works much better than giving out a home phone number, pager number, or cell phone number, because the person calling will feel more comfortable calling your office in the evening or on the weekend than calling some other number. If you have a toll-free number in your office, as I do, people can call you at any time from any place. Finally, using only an office number means that people have just one number to remember, and they don't even have to remember that if they call information or go to your Web site and get your main number, and then are led to your extension by the usual prompts.

I also carry a personal data assistant with wireless e-mail. So many people have become dependent on e-mail that, realistically, we can't go more than a couple of hours, at least during the workday, without checking e-mail and getting back to people. The wireless e-mail systems allow you to do that during breaks in meetings, while you are waiting at a traffic light, or from your kitchen table if you stay home to have breakfast with the children. It is all about being accessible and staying in contact. Your project will go more quickly and more smoothly if you do not get into telephone tag and the new variation of that, e-mail tag. Finally, most of the time nothing comes in on these electronic devices in the evening or on weekends, and when all is quiet, I can rest easy, knowing that no one is out there frustrated in their attempts to reach me. So, instead of this being intrusive, I find it gives me peace of mind.

Honesty Is the Best Policy

You may fool a commissioner or a planning staff member once, but you're unlikely to get away with it twice. Moreover, if you get caught pulling a fast one, it will take you a long time to get over that reputation. This is a lecture that you, as a grown-up, probably feel you don't need to hear, but I see it again and again—land developers and real estate investors (most of them not my clients) frustrated in their efforts to succeed in their zoning campaigns because they have a reputation for trying to play a little fast with local officials.

It is much better to say, "I simply don't know. I will get you that information as soon as I can." You will do better in the long run by saying, "I know how important it is to you that you increase the amount of open space in the town, but I simply can't do it with this project." If you say instead, "I will see what I can do. Maybe we can switch some things around," all you will do is to delay the inevitable and raise expectations that will have to be lowered.

If you are asked for information and giving it would be contrary to an agreement you have with someone else or would be damaging to your objectives at this stage in the project approval, you need to simply tell the person who is asking you that you can't share all of the information at this time, but that you will do so just as soon as, and, of course, if, you can. Tell the person that you appreciate her need to have that information now, but you have obligations to other people and have made promises that you must keep. Or tell her that you have responsibilities that transcend her interest in getting full information at this time. Neighbors and local officials can understand that. They don't understand half-truths that are later discovered to be such.

If you find a mistake in your application or you find that your representation on some important issue was wrong, do exactly what I was trained to do in pilot training: When you are lost, climb, confess, and communicate. You need to get above the problem and get some perspective, you need to start talking to people, and you need to confess the error. Fessing up is the hardest thing to do—and almost always the best solution when you find out you are wrong.

Recently, we had been working on a very difficult and contentious case involving a state's jurisdiction over tidal waters. We had the best scientists, engineers, and surveyors working on the problem, and we had presented an ironclad case for our position. Just a couple of weeks after we filed our petition for a declaratory ruling, our chief scientist reported back to us that the federal government figures on which he had based his analysis had been corrected by the government and were somewhat less desirable for us.

This obviously wasn't our fault. It was the federal government that had amended its own data. The new data might not be discovered by the state. What should we do?

We immediately notified the state government authorities with whom we had filed the motion for the declaratory ruling and submitted a modified motion with the new data. As a consequence, we suffered a 30-day delay in the proceedings. Our scientist was less than pleased, an opponent razzed us a little, our client understood (fortunately), and we knew that in the long run, it would serve our client's interests. As lawyers, we were almost certainly ethically obligated to reveal the information to the government agency, so the decision wasn't hard to make. Not all ethical situations are this clear cut, but it is almost always better to reveal new information if it is relevant to the decision-making process.

Maintaining Confidentiality

An important part of maintaining and leveraging relationships to reach your zoning objectives is maintaining confidentiality. You need to be trusted, and you need to be able to trust other people.

A great deal of damage can be done when the possibility of a project leaks out prematurely. A recent newspaper article talked about a landowner who was reported to have entered into an agreement to sell a highly visible property to an out-of-state developer. The reporter called the chief elected official of the community, who said that he didn't know anything about it, but that he was concerned about the development of this key parcel. This is not a good start for getting local approvals for a development project. You can't expect the chief elected official to be an avid supporter of your project if he is left out of the loop.

In the military, access to information is based on an individual's clearance and, importantly, his "need to know." While it is important for you to keep everybody on your development team up to speed, you should limit the information you give to team members to only what they need to know. The less information there is out there, the less chance there is that something will be intentionally or inadvertently communicated prematurely.

I realized a long time ago that it is much better for me and for my wife if I don't talk about my cases with her. Although she is a lawyer and is scrupulous in maintaining confidentiality, it is not fair to put her in the position of trying to remember what she is supposed to know and what she is not supposed to know.

It is the same whether you are a real estate investor or developer, or anyone else involved in the business of land use and zoning, including a member of an interest group or neighborhood organization that may be opposed to particular developments. Maintaining confidentiality and keeping critical information secure are of the utmost importance.

Do not depend on written confidentiality agreements between sellers and buyers, or between developers and their consultants, to give you the protection you need. I had one instance where we were secretly buying a social club in order to include it as part of a potential expansion of an abutting office project. The deal was subject to a strict confidentiality agreement, under which neither the seller nor the buyer was to reveal the existence of the option.

You can imagine the gist of the next part of the story. Several months into the deal, I received a call from an architect I knew who was a member of the social club and had a friend on the board. That friend on the board apparently had told him about the deal, and the architect was calling me to see if he could get the contract to design the expanded center—so much for confidentiality agreements. You should use them, but don't depend on them.

You might use a layered approach to protecting information. You might want to use one entity to create a subsidiary organization that enters into an agreement with a third entity, which actually gets control of the property. You might use multiple entities to assemble land. The purpose is not to be devious or deceitful, but to protect information about ownership, control, and the plan from being revealed to the wrong people at the wrong time. Ultimately, your project and the zoning objectives you are seeking in furtherance of the project will become self-evident. But until that time, and as part of maintaining solid relationships with the people involved in the deal, with the public, and with the governmental decision makers, you need to control and protect essential information.

Maintaining confidentiality is a critical part of maintaining and leveraging relationships. If the mayor tells you something in confidence, you shouldn't share that information with the planner or the economic development commission. At the same time, to maintain and make effective use of your relationships, you should not create an untenable situation by giving confidential information to someone who is duty-bound to report it to someone else. A real estate investor should not tell a county planner that she might delay the start of the project for a few months while she does "a little environmental remediation" if she is not prepared to reveal that to the agency for which the planner works and from which the developer intends to receive site plan approval. It may be information that it is important for the planner to know, and the real estate investor may have good reasons for not wanting any public discussion about it, but giving such confidential information to the planner leaves the planner in an unnecessarily difficult situation.

Sometimes the government wants information from us that we can't give up because it is proprietary or might compromise site security. One way to handle this is to make an agreement with the government to have a third party serve as an intermediary. That third party might be a member of the government staff or might be an outside consultant. Subject to freedom of information laws, you may be able to enter into a confidentiality agreement with that third party. The information is provided to the third party, who then analyzes it and ultimately reports to the government authority, with an assessment as to whether there has been compliance with the law.

Partisan Politics

Partisan politics may be helpful at the state level in some states and may be helpful at the local level, particularly in larger cities, but for the most part, partisan politics is not controlling in smaller municipalities. Yes, partisan politics must be respected. Where you believe that party politics is strong in a municipality, you may benefit from talking to the party chair at some point.

Hardball politics of the machine variety usually is not going to determine the outcome of your zoning campaigns. In short, don't depend on politics, at least of the partisan variety, to get what you want out of zoning, unless you are in one of those big cities where the "political machine" is at work.

Creating, maintaining, and then using these relationships in your zoning campaigns is one of the most satisfying aspects of what you need to do to get your zoning. These relationships become ends in themselves, not just a means to getting your zoning. Many of the consultants, the staffs, the elected and appointed officials, the expert witnesses, even the neighborhood gadflies who show up at every hearing to ask impossible questions may eventually become your friends. Value and respect these relationships, even though you may not always agree with some of these people. Someday these relationships will help you get what you want from zoning.

Chapter 9

Reach Out for Support

Friendships are fun, and you can leverage them into helping you along the way, but you need much more leverage than those one-on-one friendships can provide.

Remember our planning paradigm? You need to know what you have, what you want, and how to get it.

Similarly, you need to know who is out there and what their attitudes are, you need to know what you can reasonably expect to get from them, and you need to have a plan for marshaling that support.

Finding out who is out there and what they're thinking can be done in several ways. Sometimes a telephone survey will reveal community preferences. Focus groups can often be helpful in discerning community attitudes. Later on, when more information on the project is out in the open, you might want to hold neighborhood or community meetings to describe the project and get public input, although I must say that you should have little or no expectation that you will convert opponents into proponents. I like neighborhood meetings, and I frequently use them. When you finally arrive in front of the public decision makers, it is helpful that they know that you have reached out to the community and made an attempt to get its support. But the plain fact is that most community meetings are not used by opponents to open their minds to the merits of your proposal, but rather to gather information that will be useful in defeating your project.

It can be highly productive to review the files of previous zoning proceedings, contentious and otherwise. Local governments are required to keep files, and you may be able to get a sense of what will happen with your project by looking at what happened with a prior one. You can use one of the Internet search engines to get newspaper articles and reported decisions involving prior projects.

We have discovered an interesting phenomenon in researching prior controversial projects. When neighborhoods have opposed development projects, almost invariably, once the project is up and operating, it so blends into the existing fabric of the community that even some of its strongest opponents will concede that the project is a good one. You can get a great boost for your project if you can get one of these prior opponents to come out in support of your project. It doesn't happen often, but it is worth the effort.

If you do a good reconnaissance of what the public wants, I guarantee that in almost every instance you will be surprised at your own misperceptions of what is important to the community. I don't care if you have done every kind of project all over this country, as I have, or if you are the consummately sensitive local real estate investor who has been uniformly successful in getting your project through zoning; good survey work will reveal information that will greatly benefit your zoning campaign.

I was doing an expansion of a super-regional shopping mall for one of the country's premier shopping mall developers and owners. We absolutely had the best team of consultants. The company's real estate manager was among the best. He knew this business like no one else.

When we made our list of issues that we would need to address in order to win over strenuous neighborhood opposition, we put traffic at the top. The area was already congested, there was increasing retail development all around, and a substantial portion of the traffic didn't use the limited-access state highway or the immediately adjacent interstate highway, but ended up on a two-lane road through the residential neighborhood on one side of the project. That same neighborhood group had been successful in defeating an office project on the mall site some years before (before the company's real estate manager was given control of the project and before we were retained).

As part of the project, because the site was almost fully developed already, the company was going to convert some of the surface parking to structured parking. Structured parking is parking in multilevel garages. Although we knew there might be some concerns about this somewhat urban density in the suburban context, we did not believe that there would be any other issues with the structured parking.

Traffic was number one on our list, and structured parking was about number six.

Guess what the survey evidence revealed after our researchers made thousands of telephone calls and held numerous focus group meetings? Traffic was number four or five on the list of concerns, and structured parking was number one, solely because of the public's belief that it would be less safe to be in those garages than in the surface parking. The residents of the two host towns were worried about their personal safety.

We knew that there was no actual safety issue with regard to structured parking. We had the statistics, and we had all of the police reports. We knew that the potential for assaults or carjackings was actually less at the mall than in the driveways of individual homes in the host communities. In the history of the mall, dating back 25 years, there had never even been a carjacking (until, as luck would have it, some nutcase faked a carjacking at the time the hearings were going on, apparently to make a false insurance claim). The crime rate was extremely low, and security was outstanding. The mall owner and the two host towns were rightly pleased with their outstanding security record at this exceptional shopping center. Yet the public's perception—and perception is everything—was that the structured parking would compromise security.

Incidentally, here is a practice pointer on crime statistics for your development projects. If you looked at the raw numbers for incidents and police calls at the mall, they seemed substantial. When you broke those numbers down, however, they were nearly all instances of credit card fraud, with a few of the expected shoplifting cases. They were quite ordinary for any retail center. Over the history of this facility, there had been very few crimes against persons and very few crimes against property in the parking lot. The neighbors tried to use the raw crime statistics, but the zoning boards in the host towns quickly saw through that.

As a consequence of this revelation about the public's security concerns, we completely changed our presentation for the zoning hearings. We talked with the police chiefs in both towns, and one of the police chiefs testified at the hearing about the town's pride in the public safety record at the mall and why security would not be an issue. We also put on the company's chief of security, an impressive former Los Angeles Police Department officer, who explained all of the measures that would be taken to ensure security, including lighting, call boxes, and frequent patrols. On top of that, our client agreed to put in a police substation at the mall and to pay the cost of an additional police officer.

The issue of mall security and structured parking evaporated, and the towns approved the expansion. A premier department store was added to the mall, the first one of the chain in the six-state region, and numerous other stores also came to the mall, all with spectacular economic success. Had we not taken the time to assess the community's sentiments and concerns, we would never have discovered the misperception about security. It is unlikely that we would have ever addressed it in the way we did so as to eliminate it as an issue in the zoning campaign.

Grass-Tops Organizing

Grass-tops organizing is one of the best ways to answer the second question, what you can reasonably expect in terms of support when you reach out to those who may be your allies.

You are doubtless familiar with grassroots organizing, principally from the environmental movement. The idea is that if you can get lots of people, lots of ordinary people, all across the country to support your position, you will rise in strength from the grass roots all the way up.

In the lobbying, community organizing, and zoning campaign business, we look higher than the grass roots; we go to that stratum at the local level where we find the opinion leaders. The opinion leaders may include former elected officials, members of the clergy, prominent businesspeople, folks who are known for their philanthropy, and perhaps someone with celebrity or local hero status, such as a war veteran or sports star.

If you can involve these opinion leaders in your project early on and give them a meaningful role in shaping the project, they can be extraordinarily helpful in getting your zoning approved and marketing your project. I learned best how to do this from a great developer, Mark Steiner, who put together a grass-tops focus group, perhaps better described as an advisory committee, for a mixed-residential-use continuum-of-care project.

The project was targeted to empty-nesters and seniors and would provide a mix of housing, from age-restricted single-family detached housing through apartments and ownership condominiums, assisted living, and ultimately skilled nursing. The project was adjacent to an established residential neighborhood of moderate-density single-family detached homes.

This advisory committee included community leaders, most of them older and all of them highly regarded. Their critique of the early project concepts was helpful in shaping the project. In the end, not simply because of this committee, but also because of outreach to the surrounding neighborhood, the density on the site was doubled. Multistory buildings were approved, and all of the zoning was ultimately granted unanimously by the council, with no opposition at the public hearing. This is truly a remarkable result, driven largely by the developer's foresight in involving community leaders, listening to their good advice, and then going to the hearing with their support.

Turning the Opposition into Supporters

Don't expect to turn your opponents into allies in most cases. But if you're willing to reach out to the opposition, to listen to them, to respect their views, and to respond to their reasonable concerns, you may be able to neutralize some of them and even turn a few to your side.

Sometimes opposition is based on misinformation. Neighbors, for example, are often appropriately concerned about delivery trucks at nearby proposed retail facilities. If you give them a schedule of those deliveries and document from other facilities that the schedule is routinely observed, that may be enough to end the opposition.

When delivery traffic seems to be a key issue, developers will sometimes eliminate the opposition by limiting the delivery traffic to certain hours. We had one gas station where we agreed that the delivery tankers would come only during nighttime hours, when there would be no schoolchildren around, and we noted as part of the restriction that in the event of bad weather, such as a snowstorm, the delivery truck might be delayed and might need to deliver outside of the agreed-upon times. The neighbors understood this and had no objection to the rare exception.

Never promise something that you can't guarantee or enforce. It is reasonable for the neighbors to have the right to enforce an agreement that you make with them and, in the event that they need to enforce the agreement and you are found to be in violation, to be reimbursed for their attorneys' fees. Too generous, you say? Not at all. You should not make an agreement that you cannot keep and that you cannot enforce.

In another case, from our inquiries of the neighbors as to why they had previously opposed a new store across the street, we found that their real concern wasn't the proposed store, but the possibility that a vacant parcel at the end of their block would be developed as a branch bank, with traffic added to the nearby residential streets. They believed that building the new store across the street would make the area attractive for a bank, and that that would precipitate the sale and development of the parcel.

We turned this opposition into support by eliminating their sole objection. Our client purchased the vacant lot where the neighbors feared that a bank might go and imposed a conservation restriction on it, preserving it as open space forever. Of course, the conservation restriction was not actually placed on the lot until the retailer received full approval for its development and no appeal was taken. The timing of a restriction is a powerful incentive for the opposition to support the project. No support, no approval, no restriction.

Here's a suggestion that other people in the zoning business may find to be foolish, but my developer clients and I have used it with great success many times. It arises from the classic David-and-Goliath scenario. The big corporate developer, with its team of experts and experienced legal advisers, proposes a project. The vocal, sophisticated, and money-starved neighborhood group opposes the project because of the neighbors' concerns about the new traffic, and the group says: "We're just a little neighborhood group. We own our modest houses, and we struggle to make ends meet. The big developer has all of these fancy consultants and expensive lawyers. This is unfair. We can't do our own traffic studies and get legal advice, because we can't afford it. We are David, and they are Goliath."

I've heard this dozens of times over the years, and it is essentially truthful, though a little dramatic. What to do?

We have been successful in most instances in eliminating opposition or turning opposition into support in this type of situation by offering to pay the cost of experts retained by the neighborhood group, even a lawyer. We reserve the right to veto the choice of any consultant or lawyer, because we want to be sure that the opposition retains only highly qualified people. There are more than enough excellent consultants and lawyers who work in this area, so that a veto over their selection does not measurably reduce the opportunities for the neighborhood group. We also usually cap the fees, although there have been instances in which we have then increased the caps as necessary.

For example, in doing an office project next to a residential condominium, the developer client found it necessary to undertake extensive blasting. Blasting is a difficult issue for all concerned. The neighbors are almost always worried that their property will be damaged, and the developer ought to be worried that someone nearby who has had a foundation crack for 20 years is going to believe that it somehow resulted from the blasting. Before our clients blast, we enter into an extensive agreement with the neighbors, including bonding for the cost of any repairs and performing preblast and postblast inspections. More often than not, neighbors want their own engineer to assess the blasting plan and to participate in the surveys before or after blasting. We budgeted for the engineering consultant and lawyer hired by the condominium. The project went through some unexpected changes and delays. Our client found it necessary over several years to increase the cap for the engineer and the lawyer hired by the condominium because of the changes and delay.

Importantly, the condominium supported the project at the public hearings and in several reapplications, extensions, and amendments. The developer would not have had the condominium's support had it not completely addressed the neighbors' concerns and supported the independent review by a qualified engineer and lawyer, which gave these neighbors the comfort they needed to know that the project would be done correctly and safely.

Show Me the Money

Sometimes it's all about money.

Let's put one aspect of money right on the table and be done with it. Paying local officials, directly or indirectly, is illegal; you can go to jail for it, and it is wrong. Don't even think about it. I know of a land-use planner working for a municipality who was convicted for having taken money indirectly from a developer. Indirect payments are the most sinister because they can appear acceptable to some misguided people. It is just as illegal to sell the mayor's daughter a condominium for $10,000 less than the market as it is to give the mayor $10,000 cash.

But how about paying the neighbors? That's a different story.

You may recall the case I mentioned in Chapter 5 where the corporation paid the neighbors to release a restriction that benefited them so that the company could break up the corporate headquarters into multiple offices. This is entirely legal, ethical, proper, and simply good business practice. Having the restriction benefited those neighbors, and they were compensated for the negotiated value of the restriction that they gave up with the release.

If your project's neighbors, either adjoining or nearby, claim and can prove that their property will be substantially devalued as a consequence of your development, it may be time to think about either purchasing those properties, which we have done in many cases, or paying the neighbors for their loss in value.

In nearly every case, a legitimate appraisal will show that an intensification of development in the area has no measurable impact on value. In fact, surrounding properties often increase in value because your project will make them more attractive for more intensive development. Why, they should be paying you!

Sometimes we approach the surrounding owners before we announce a project and offer to purchase their properties, usually at a slight premium. This enables the neighbors to move to a new place if they don't like the idea of more intensive development going in nearby. Sometimes the neighbors use this as an opportunity to move to larger or smaller quarters. Yes, this costs money, but let's suppose you are going to put up a new store, and that store will make you $1 million a year in profit. If you can speed up the approval process, avoid appeals to the courts, and save a year's time in permitting, you actually have up to $1 million to spend on offsetting the impacts in the neighborhood.

If it cost you $200,000 to take care of three or four residential properties nearby, you are ahead by $800,000. More importantly, with many development projects, the first ones to get up and operating will seize the market, whether it is for retail or office use, and you will foreclose competition. A delay in your project could kill it if someone gets in ahead of you. Getting your project done quickly may increase its profitability, not only because of the normal return over a longer period, but also because you have captured a segment of the market and have foreclosed entry by others.

Often the purchased properties can be resold at no loss or even at a premium. The properties may be incorporated into your development and later rezoned to allow expansion of your project.

Discussions with the neighbors about buying their property sometimes backfire big time. Neighbors often believe that they have leverage over your project and demand high premiums. I had one where a modest ranch house was worth maybe $100,000; the owner claimed it was worth $250,000. Our client eventually bought him out and moved him, but it was a difficult and expensive process.

You can protect and enhance the value of neighboring property, thereby eliminating opposition. You can offer a new fence or landscaping. In one project, as we often do, we drew height-of-eye perspectives from the kitchen windows of all the surrounding houses where they looked into the proposed development. We wanted to make sure that views were protected where they could be protected, and we needed information to share with the neighbors about what they were likely to see of the development. We thought this would help to demonstrate to the public decision makers that we had made every effort to minimize the impact. When one of the designers talked with an elderly woman at her house, she said how much she liked looking at this big tree in her backyard, and she hoped it would not be damaged. One problem: The tree wasn't in her backyard, it was on our client's property, and it was in the location of a proposed manhole for part of the drainage system. The tree had to go if the drainage system was to be constructed as designed. The developer, Mark Steiner, whom I mentioned earlier, directed the engineers to redesign the drainage system to relocate the catch basin. It required an extra manhole and cost a few thousand dollars, but it made an abutter a supporter who spoke in favor of the project.

This concept of looking carefully at the potential adverse impacts on the neighbors sends a powerful message to neighbors and government officials. It says that you care about doing the right thing, and that you are not afraid of the facts. It says that you want to identify all of the impacts, and that you are prepared to mitigate them where it is practical to do so. No one can ask for more than that—at least, not without being unreasonable.

We were helping a major retailer develop a multistate distribution facility in an industrial zone, but close to a small residential neighborhood of a few houses. Part of the warehouse would be 50 feet high. We imagined that if we were a residential neighbor of this proposed facility, we would want to know what we could see from our house. Using a technique that has proved effective in the past, we sent out one of our law firm's environmental analysts with a large red weather balloon on a 50-foot line. The land surveyor helped us locate the corners of the tallest part of the building and double-checked the elevation on the ground so that we were sure that the balloon would be tethered exactly to the height of the proposed building. Our analyst photographed the balloon from all angles, including the direct view from the house that was closest to the project and from the end of the residential street closest to the project. The photographs revealed that all but a small part of the building would be totally hidden behind trees. We then asked to meet with each of the homeowners in his or her home. We showed the homeowners the plans of the facility; talked about the schedule of construction; discussed the nature of the operation, including employment and traffic; and showed them with the weather balloon photographs what they would be likely to see from their homes and from the end of their street.

Only one of the neighbors showed up at the hearing, and he said nothing. He was apparently satisfied with our efforts. The project was unanimously approved in a short six weeks, with no opposition and no appeals. That is worth the cost of a walk in the woods with a weather balloon on a 50-foot line and visits with a few homeowners.

Rather than install fences or landscaping on neighboring properties to temper the impact of a new development, we sometimes design the fences and landscaping, develop very generous budget figures, and then offer the neighbors the alternative of installing the improvements themselves. I will tell you that 9 times out of 10, when homeowners elect to make the improvements themselves, we give them checks after all approvals and appeals, and no improvements are ever made. That is fine, because it is their choice.

The improvements can often be substantial. In one strip center project with a large anchor supermarket, our client created an enormous earthen berm (an elongated hill) to block the view of the open center from the surrounding residential neighborhood.

The project itself can be changed to eliminate the impacts on the surrounding properties and turn opposition into support. Developers have screened rooftop heating, ventilation, and air conditioning systems; installed low-noise systems, completely enclosed loading docks; and brought trash compactors inside.

Opposition may not be stopped before a hearing or during a hearing or even after a hearing. Opposition that remains after an approval can lead to a court appeal. Even when a project is approved and the neighbors appeal it, there is still an opportunity to change that opposition into support. The project can be altered, the neighbors' properties can be buffered with fences and landscaping, and money payments can be made. The payment may compensate the neighbors for the alleged adverse impacts and reimburse them for their expenses in opposing the project.

There are some legal and ethical limits. In rare cases, the demands of the opponents in settling litigation exceed reasonableness. Real estate investors and developers who are caught up in such cases must simply decide whether it is worth it to pay excessive amounts to be rid of litigation.

Unfortunately, there are many creative ways to sue someone. Although a lawyer and plaintiff must have probable cause for starting an action, this does not mean that their case needs to have great merit. Lawsuits may be nearly frivolous and still stop a project completely. Few lenders are interested in lending large sums of money for development projects that might not be able to be occupied or, worse yet, might have to be torn down if the developer loses in litigation. There are few instances where we can predict with certainty the outcome of litigation, and because of that risk, no matter how remote it may be, many projects are rendered unfinanceable during litigation.

One of the best ways to cut off opposition directed at exacting money from the developer is to have the stomach and the resources to go forward with the project with the approvals, even though those approvals have been challenged in court. While a challenger may try to get an injunction to stop your project, in most cases they will not get it, especially if you're prepared to fund the cost of removing the improvements and restoring the site. We have had several projects go forward during the appeals, particularly when the project will make enough money during the appeals to completely pay for itself. We had that with a fast-food restaurant and a gas station. They both were projected to be profitable enough during the first year of operation, about the length of time it would take for the appeal to run its course in court, to justify the cost of construction with an amount set aside to demolish the buildings and restore the sites. This is the exception, however. Most projects cannot go forward during litigation.

Opposition may be driven by more altruistic objectives. A group may be opposing your residential subdivision because it does not provide for affordable housing or because the group believes that the development will contribute to sprawl. This group might be persuaded to withdraw its opposition or withdraw a judicial appeal if you support its charitable objectives. You could do this by developing affordable housing elsewhere or by facilitating a denser, new urbanist community on another site. You could also do it by making a contribution to one or more charitable organizations that produce affordable housing or encourage smart growth. You might create a trust fund to disburse funds for those types of charitable activities.

Your project does not have to be the one where the issues are addressed or resolved. It may be that your residential subdivision should go forward as an exclusive, expensive gated community of mansion homes. Somewhere else in the community, you may find a location for affordable housing, purchase open space, save a farm by buying conservation easements over it, or fund the creation of a new plan and new regulations for new urbanist development. The point is that you do not necessarily have to give up your project in order to settle with the opposition.

One final note on getting support for your project: While it takes the personal touch of calling people, meeting with them, and addressing their individual needs, for larger projects, where the stakes are high and the size warrants it, you should have professional help. You'll need a public relations consultant to assist you in presenting your project to the media and to help with your Web site. You will need marketing professionals to identify the views of the community. The strategists who manage political campaigns can be very helpful in local zoning work. You need to get the public to vote for your project, just like a candidate needs enough votes to win. Our larger and most successful zoning campaigns have been planned and implemented with the help of political strategists and have been run more like campaigns for public office. Ultimately, the merits of the project must carry the day. But how you shape the development, determine the key elements of your message, communicate to constituents, and bring the elected and appointed officials to vote for your project is political in the best sense of that process.

Chapter 10

Preparing Winning Applications

The last step in getting ready to make your move is to prepare the best application you can. The application, like the planning process, requires you to know what you have, what you want, and how to get it.

The application must be complete and accurate. It should have an executive summary at the beginning so that anyone who picks it up will know, at least generally, what you're proposing to do without having to dig through a volume of material. While it is difficult to put too much in an application, what you do submit should be organized, and you should provide enough copies to meet the government's needs.

The first introduction of your project to the decision makers, at least in the formal part of getting your zoning, is probably going to be through this application. If it is sloppy, with typographic errors, mark-overs, and incomplete sections, all you have managed to do is tell everyone at the outset that you are ill prepared and someone that they may have trouble trusting.

On the other hand, if the application is complete, well written, neat, and businesslike in its appearance and organization, you will have gone far toward getting your approval. Remember, your application is going to be distributed to the decision makers before the meeting or hearing and may be distributed to other local government staff. It will be distributed to regional officials in some cases, and your potential opposition is likely to go to the local government offices to read it. Your application "speaks" to dozens of people, long before your hearing.

Do not include materials in odd formats that are not readily reproducible in a later record. Large sheets, foldouts, exhibits in color, and submissions on other than paper media, such as photographic slides and computer disks, are not going to be able to be viewed by everyone who may need to see them. If there is an appeal, and you are in a state where the appeal is based totally on the record, it may be the judge who cannot read what you have to say in your application.

Your first step in preparing an excellent application is to ask the staff for permission to see examples of applications that they think are particularly good. These applications do not have to be from similar projects, although that might be helpful. Suppose you need that variance for the above-ground pool we talked about in Chapter 7. You've never done a variance, and you have no idea what should be in an application. If you study a dozen variance applications, paying particular attention to the ones that the staff says were done well, it will be as if you had made a dozen variance applications before, some that were highly successful and some that you made mistakes on and learned from.

The staff would rather spend time with you at the preapplication stage to get the application as right as it can be than have to reject it as incomplete and put you (and them!) through the process of starting over. It's the old business of, if you don't have time to do it right the first time, you don't have time to redo it or fix it.

You may also request a preapplication meeting with the board or agency. At the preapplication stage, you do not have any property interest at stake, and the rules for procedural due process do not apply. In most jurisdictions there does not have to be any notice of a preapplication meeting other than the posting of the agenda, at least not the same notice as you would have for an application and hearing. A preapplication meeting is quite informal. It is basically a short presentation by you about what you are thinking of applying for and a request that the board give you some guidance in preparing your application.

Unfortunately, many final decision makers are wary of preapplication meetings and simply won't have them. They have been burned once too often by people who have had preapplication meetings and then, after the application has been filed, hammered them with comments they may have made in the informal and nonbinding preapplication meeting.

In most cases, once you have filed the application and are in the formal process, it would be unwise to refer back to any preapplication discussions. The staff and the public officials who are deciding on your application are not going to be forthcoming with you and offer candid comments at the preapplication stage if they believe you may try to gain some advantage during the formal process by attempting to hold them to positions they may have taken early on.

If you're not a particularly good writer, have a friend who is better at writing review the rough draft of your application. Ask her if she understands it fully and if she will edit your draft. You are probably too close to your situation to see where you may have skipped over an important detail. It is like trying to balance your checkbook when you can't find the 12-cent error, but someone else looking at it sees it at once.

During the preparation of your application, you should identify any evidentiary materials that you need to include in the application or have ready in time for the hearing. If you fail to have all the evidence available, those who are opposing your application can complain with some legitimacy at the time of the public hearing that they were disadvantaged by not being able to view a complete application after the first public notice. Even if you have to put off your submission by a month or two to get the application truly complete, you will save time in the long run. You will avoid the risk that the board or agency will order you to reapply and again give notice of the application because the application that you filed was not sufficiently complete to allow the opposition to fully review the proposal and prepare for the hearing.

Here is one practice pointer, however, that may seem contrary to the recommendation of making sure you have a complete application. As we shall see in Chapter 14 on making your hearing presentation, you may gain a tactical advantage by holding back some of the details until the public hearing so that your adversaries won't have the benefit of having studied the information for several weeks in advance of the hearing. The state statutes, the local regulations, and the application form itself together should give you sufficient guidance to know what must be of record at the time of the first public notice. The supplemental information that you present at the time of the public hearing or late in the public hearing in rebuttal to the opposition is in addition to what is required as part of the application.

A notice problem can arise if the supplemental information presented during the public hearing differs substantially from what was in the application or provides great additional detail, and there is no reason why that information could not have been provided with the original application. For example, if you include a rudimentary traffic report with your application, and then you put a traffic engineer on at the hearing with large volumes of data and inconsistent information about trip generation and distribution, you risk having the hearing continued for an additional session, with the opposition having perhaps as much as a month between the sessions of the public hearing to prepare its rebuttal. Worse yet, there is usually no requirement that the opponents submit their rebuttal testimony prior to the reconvening of the continued hearing. This turns the tables on you and puts you at a disadvantage.

Furthermore, as we shall see in Part VI on opposition strategies, the powerful advantage that opponents have is that they generally do not need to submit anything in advance of the public hearing.

When you prepare an application, you should also outline for your own use the process for getting any other needed permits at the federal, state, and local level. This list should include a timeline for submission, hearing, and decision on each required approval and a sequencing plan. Some laws require applications to different boards and agencies to be submitted in a set sequence. If you reverse that sequence, you almost certainly will have to start all over again. If some opposition group has already begun to work against you and you cannot turn the group in favor of your project, being forced to withdraw and start over again because of a simple mistake in the timing or sequencing of your applications could kill your project. During the hiatus while you are reapplying, the opposition group just might convince the local legislative body to change the zoning for your land, with the likely effect that your project is no longer a permitted use. Far-fetched? Not at all. I've seen it happen to investors and developers, and I've done it to others when I was working on the opposition side.

We hardly ever have sleepless nights with our zoning applications. In this area of the law, although the financial stakes may be high, we generally are not dealing with life-and-death issues. But if there is anything that raises our level of anxiety, it is that we might make a mistake in the timing or sequencing of applications or inadvertently submit an incomplete application that is rejected on that ground alone, and thus give the opposition a chance to slip in and pull the zoning rug out from underneath our client's project.

Something like that happened to a developer in a case where the public notice of the hearing was required to be published in the newspaper and posted on a sign on the property. The city had wanted to reduce the residential density in that area and was in the process of amending the zoning ordinance to cut the density in half. The subdivision application, however, had made it in under the wire and was being processed under the existing, higher-density regulations, when it was discovered that the posted notice on the property had the wrong date. The notice failed, and the subdivision hearing could not go forward. The project application had to be refiled, and, by the time this was done, the zoning had been amended, wiping out half the number of lots.

The developer sued his lawyer for malpractice, and I was called as an expert witness on the standard of care for the preparation and posting of the sign. The point of the story is a simple one: Although in most zoning cases, you can start over again when you make a mistake, in the most controversial ones, there is a very real chance that your project will be either damaged or destroyed while you fix a procedural error. Just like the old adage in carpentry of "measure twice, cut once," you need to double-check and triple-check timelines, sequencing, and the list of all necessary applications to make sure that you have minimized the chances of error.

Notices

More zoning litigation arises out of procedural problems, including notice issues, than out of anything else. A zoning application is a matter of administrative law, and in most states the procedural requirements are strictly construed. That is, a court is not going to cut you any slack when it comes to following what the statutes and regulations require, especially as to notice.

The law varies so much from state to state and municipality to municipality that there is not much that can be said generally. You need to start by reading the state statutes. If you are in a municipality with a charter, you will need to read that as well, because the provisions of the charter may vary from those of the state enabling statute.

Outline the procedural requirements, including the particulars of the notice required and the timing for submission, notice, and action on your zoning application.

Public notice often requires notice in a newspaper of general circulation. If you have this requirement in your state, you are probably going to want to look at a newspaper in which most of the public notices are published. Again, the planning staff can help you. It may be that the municipality publishes the notice itself, which is often the case, and you will have nothing to do with that process.

If the municipality is going to draft and publish the notice (and charge you for it), you will probably want to participate in some way in that process. We see many instances in which the notice was incomplete or inaccurate because of inadvertent staff error. You might ask to review the notice as drafted before it is sent to the newspaper.

Most notice requirements direct that the notice include a brief description of the application, such as: "special permit application for a day-care center in the R-2 zone for fewer than 20 children." The description must be sufficient to apprise the public of the general nature of the proposal.

If you are going to amend the ordinance, in some jurisdictions, you will have to publish the entire amendment verbatim. In other jurisdictions, it may be sufficient to generally describe the nature of the amendment.

Most jurisdictions require that you identify the property with particularity, and the majority of notice cases are ones in which the street address was wrong. Maybe the street address listed was the side street instead of the street frontage or the address was completely wrong, but the name of the property owner was correct. Often the legal street address may be different from the street address that is generally used, as many businesses at street intersections prefer to use the street address on the main street, rather than the legal address on the side street. Double-check the address of your property given in the application and make sure that it is right.

The owner's and applicant's names may both need to be listed, or maybe only one of the two is needed. Regardless, they must be correct. Sometimes with multiple business entities and limited liability corporations, problems in figuring out who is the owner and who is the applicant actually arise. The information needs to be accurate, however, because sharp-eyed opponents will often check the name of the corporation with the state's secretary of the state and then claim a notice problem if the corporation's name is not exactly as it is of record with the state.

The time, date, and place of the public hearing must be exactly correct. If the time of the public hearing is listed as 7:30 p.m., and the public hearing actually starts at 7:00 p.m., you have a problem. Someone can claim that he did not show up until the published time of 7:30 p.m., and that his procedural due process rights were violated because the hearing proceeded without him.

You need to check to make sure that the notice is published in the newspaper as required. We have seen numerous instances where newspaper's staff dropped the ball and the newspaper either didn't publish the notice at all or didn't publish it on the day required. Notice requirements typically direct that the newspaper notice be published a certain number of days, usually within a range of dates, before the public hearing. If the notice is not published at all or in a timely manner, the hearing will have to be delayed. In most states, you can republish the notice and simply start the clock running again.

If, for whatever reason, the notice as published is wrong in some way, the best thing to do in most jurisdictions is to republish a corrected notice and start the time clock over. You generally will not have to withdraw and reapply, but you will almost certainly have to select a later date for the public hearing.

If the notice requirements provide that the property be posted with a sign, not only will the content need to be just as correct as that in the newspaper notice, but the size of the sign and its location on the property will also need to be correct. Even the size of the letters may be specified. The regulations may require that the sign be on the property continuously for a certain number of days prior to the hearing. This turns out to be the problem we encounter most often. Vandals (or dare I say the opposition?) may knock down or steal the sign. If the requirement is that the sign be up continuously and it disappears for a couple of days until you can put it back, you may have a notice problem. Consequently, where it is critical that we not have a notice problem or where we believe we may have difficulties in maintaining the sign continuously on the property, we will have one or two extra signs made up and available for immediate installation. We will have someone check the property at least once a day and replace the sign if it disappears. We maintain a log of those checks of the sign so that we can verify that the sign was up there every day of the notice period.

It is often required that notice be sent to abutting property owners or those within a certain distance of the property boundary. When notices are sent by mail, certified mail, return receipt requested is often used, so that you will receive green postcards from the U.S. Postal Service to submit to the staff on or before the commencement of the public hearing as proof that the letters were sent and received.

Sometimes regulations mistakenly say that the letters should be sent by registered mail. Registered mail is required when you need a chain of custody for the item being put in the mail, which usually occurs when the item is something of intrinsic value, like jewelry. It is not appropriate for the mailing of notices, but if that is what the regulations say, you should do it. If you do a lot of business under zoning regulations that require registered mail, it may be a good idea to request that this be changed to certified mail, return receipt requested. It may also be sufficient to simply have a certificate of mailing without the return receipt. That is less expensive and will demonstrate that the letters were posted to the right people at the right time.

Speaking of the right people, there are many problems that arise with mailed notices. First of all, who owns the property within a certain number of feet of your property? You need to take a plan of the property and a compass, the kind with a sharp point on one end and a pencil on the other, and scribe all around your property, set at the distance of the notice requirement. You will get an odd shape with curves at the specified number of feet from the corners of your property, but this is one way to do it. You may want to have your engineer or surveyor do it for you, so that you are sure it is accurate. You can use the assessor's maps to identify the boundaries of the abutting and nearby properties.

Even if just a few feet of a property are within the specified distance from your boundary, you need to notify the owner.

How do you find out who the owner is? In most jurisdictions, the assessor's records are the place to go, but with people buying and selling properties all the time, those records may not be up-to-date. Good zoning regulations will specify that the assessor's records (or the city or county clerk's records) are all you need to check. In other jurisdictions, you may need to go beyond the assessor's records and even look at land titles to find out who has recently recorded a deed. This is an expensive and time-consuming process, but with big, complex projects where there is much at risk, especially when the opposition is well organized, we will do title searches on all the surrounding properties.

Notice often must be made to all of the abutting or surrounding owners, which may mean notice to multiple owners of the same property. This can be especially burdensome if you have something like a residential condominium as an abutting owner. Suppose that you have just 10 feet of the open space of a condominium with 1,000 owners abutting your development site. Arguably, under some regulations, you may need to send notice by mail to all 1,000 individual owners and the condominium association. If the regulations are not clear on this issue, ask the staff or the agency for direction before you do your notice. If the regulations are ambiguous, you can seek a minor amendment to clarify that notice to the homeowners' association is sufficient.

The regulations are likely to require that the notice be sent out some number of days before the hearing. Suppose that you are required to send the notice at least 20 days prior to the hearing. You send the notice to 32 owners within 100 feet of your property boundary, just as the regulations require. You have in hand the certificates of mailing showing that the notices were sent 21 days prior to the hearing. About a week before the hearing, you assemble the return receipts from the U.S. Postal Service, and you find that two of the notices came back indicating that the owners of two of the properties had moved and were no longer at the addresses listed in the assessor's records or never picked up the letters. Has notice failed? Will you be required to withdraw your applications and start over? Probably not. But what are you going to do?

Again, what is acceptable practice varies from place to place, but most courts will hold that reasonable attempts to reach all of the abutters are all that is required. One approach in this situation is to hand-deliver a notice to the property and to have whoever delivers it sign an affidavit that the notice was delivered and attached to the property in some way on that date. You might also want to check the land records to determine if there is a new owner, and if there is, you may want to follow up with a telephone call or some other attempt to give the new owner actual notice, even though it technically will not be timely. When the hearing starts, you can submit the receipts or, for the people who did not sign for the notice, you can put in the affidavits indicating that you posted actual notice on the properties, and you can explain what additional steps you took to try to give notice to those owners. Fortunately, in most jurisdictions, notice of this type does not have to be perfect, although it does help to show that you made reasonable attempts to follow up.

If one of the people who did not sign for the notice complains that she never got the notice (and you can't prove that she did), shows up at the hearing, and participates (usually by complaining that she didn't get the notice), you probably do not have a notice problem, because actual notice as evidenced by the neighbor's appearing and participating in the hearing is sufficient even if legal notice was not given. See, the law does make sense sometimes.

PART III

PUTTING ON YOUR CASE

Chapter 11

Know What to Expect

Do you have the sense that one of the keys to success in a zoning campaign is to be fully prepared? I hope so.

Knowing what to expect at a public hearing is essential to getting what you want from zoning. That means taking the time to prepare, and preparing starts with observing the board at work.

Once you have decided to come in with some type of zoning application and you know what board you will appear before, start attending its meetings. One night is probably not enough to give you a sense of the full range of how the board handles its business—plan on going three or four nights. This will also give you an opportunity, even before your preapplication meeting, to introduce yourself to the individual council, commission, or board members and explain why you are "mysteriously" sitting there. "Hi, I'm Robin Jones, the owner of Robin's Majestic Pizza, and I'm going to be filing an application with you to add an outdoor dining area at the rear of my restaurant. I've never been before the zoning board before, so I thought I would come and observe for a couple of evenings."

What a great way to introduce yourself and your project, and to address your concern about being fully prepared. You're looking good already.

If you've never spent time in these meetings, you may be surprised at what goes on. These are informal meetings. The board members bring their own personal experience and knowledge of the community to bear in making their decisions. This is exactly as it should be. Formal rules of evidence and courtlike presentations seem stilted and out of place—because they are. You can be businesslike without acting like a television show about lawyers. I used to laugh to myself at trial lawyers appearing in front of zoning boards when they would accidentally say "Your Honor," or "May it pleased the court," until, in arguing a case in front of a state supreme court, I accidentally referred to the court as "the commission." Oops. Habits are hard to change.

If this is the room that will be used for your hearing, look at how it is set up. You need to make sure you visit the room you will present in before the night of your hearing. The board is often at a table across the room facing the audience. The presenter needs to make the presentation to the board, but she shouldn't be forced to turn her back on the audience. That is disrespectful, and it makes it impossible to read audience reaction during the presentation. Sometimes a presenter stands at the side of the room and struggles to face the board half of the time and the audience the other half of the time. Does he stand to the side and use a pointer or laser? Or does he stand in front of the exhibit, making it impossible for the audience to see?

If you are going to show photographic slides or use a computer projection as part of your presentation, where will the screen be? Is there a place to put the projector? Will the audience be able to see the presentation at the same time as the board? If yours is a small and informal presentation, will you be able to get close enough to the members of the board to have them see your presentation and to be able to make eye contact with them?

Note things about the presentations of others that don't work well. Are the presenters prepared? Are they able to display their exhibits effectively? I guarantee that you're going to see some presenter, even a professional, such as an architect or engineer, struggle with big clips and a set of plans slipping off an easel. You'll notice how well the presentations go when the few exhibits are dry-mounted on foam panels and arranged in the order that they are presented.

Look at the appearance of some of the presenters. If somebody has a lawyer from out of town, does she look like she's ready to argue a case in the U.S. Supreme Court in her formal designer suit, while everybody else in your rural county is dressed like they just came from a tractor pull contest? On the other hand, did somebody's traffic engineer look like he selected his wardrobe at a tag sale, communicating a lack of professionalism?

And speaking of demeanor, how do the various presenters play to this board? Are they direct, or are they wordy? Do they make eye contact, or do they look down at the floor and shuffle their feet? Do they hide behind a podium, or do they step out and speak with animation? Do they try to be helpful in explaining complex issues, or do they talk down to the board?

We had one contentious case in which we were representing the board. The developer's engineer, in frustration and obvious anger after many nights of hearings, barked at a board member in response to a fair question about an exceedingly complex scientific matter: "Just exactly what is it that you don't understand?" This one statement was probably the best remembered in some 25 nights of hearings before multiple boards and commissions. It did not prejudice the board members, but it was a window into the developer's attitude and was patently disrespectful. You don't want your application and your team to be remembered for one persnickety response.

Look around the room. Is it going to be big enough for you and your supporters? If it isn't, you need to talk to the staff about the expected turnout. One of the worst things that can happen is to have 100 people show up in a room that fits only 50. We will talk later about how to handle that situation.

How long does the presentation take, both for the applicant and for the opponents? Does it look as if people thought about what they were going to say before the session, or are they shooting from the hip, apologizing along the way: "I really didn't have time to prepare, but let me say this . . .."

Did the applicant keep his presentation to a reasonable length, or did he go on far beyond what the commission needed to know? Were the opponents direct and substantive, or were they just venting? Did the board seem to get bored with any part of the presentation or simply "tune out" at some point? Did either side concede the wisdom of someone else's position with honest recognition? "I agree that there will be more traffic congestion, and I understand Mrs. Smith's concerns, but overall, we will be improving circulation in the area, particularly through the coordination of signalization along Main Street." Or did the presenter stubbornly stick to the hard line, even though you could see the board members react incredulously: "As I said previously in my testimony, there will be no adverse impact from the minor increases in traffic volumes, and any minor degradation in the level of service will be strictly within the limits of the acceptable range under the standards of the Institute of Traffic Engineers."

Observe the deliberations of the board members just as carefully as you observe the public hearing. Did you discern any agendas of individual board members? Do they decide by consensus, or are there factions on the board? Do they vote along party lines? Do they vote depending upon where they are seated? This is sometimes the case—people of like minds often sit next to each other and vote together. Sometimes you will see them whispering back and forth during the hearing and deliberations.

Do you have the names of everybody on the board? Do you know the alternates who may substitute for regular members? What do you know about them and their interests?

How does the staff relate to the board? Is the staff subservient and professionally remote, or is the staff an equal partner with the board? Do the board members rely heavily on the staff for guidance in conducting the hearing and making decisions?

How are the proceedings recorded? Is there a stenographer, or is it on tape? Will you be tied to a microphone, or will you be able to move around?

How do the board members conduct their hearings? Do they expect the presenters to stick to a fixed period of time? Do they ask questions throughout the presentation, or do they save them until the end? Do they seem to get bored with long presentations, or are they truly interested in hearing the details? Is it apparent that they have reviewed the application in advance, or do their questions suggest that they are looking at the materials for the first time? How do they handle opponents? Do they give them a fixed period of time to speak and not allow them to speak again until everyone has had a chance to speak, or do they let some individuals go on and on?

Every town, city, and county is different in how it conducts its zoning business. Every board and council is different and has its own culture. Every elected and appointed official is different because of his or her background and perspective, and you cannot read a book like this and know what to expect. You must go and observe and prepare. If you do so, you will have a highly effective presentation that meets the needs of the staff and those who will vote on it, and you will absolutely optimize your chances for getting the result you want. If you don't get the lay of the land before the night of your hearing, at the very least you may be embarrassed, and at the worst, all of your effort may be for naught.

Chapter 12

Script and Orchestrate Your Presentation

Please don't shake your head at this suggestion. Even if you are only asking for a variance for that above-ground pool, you need at least an outline of what you intend to say. Even for the most modest of applications when you are the only speaker, you may still want to give the board members a one-page outline with your name and address at the top and a description of your application: "I am requesting a variance to allow an above-ground pool in the rear yard of my lot, which was developed when the property was in a quarter-acre zone and has since been rezoned to half-acre." Your outline should also have the salient facts and argument.

In the above-ground pool case, your outline probably starts with the facts: when the house was built and the lot area, side yards, and setbacks. While the board members may already have a site plan of some type in their packages, you might want to attach a second sheet with a site plan and a third or fourth sheet with photographs of your property, probably with your daughters in one of the shots (really). A photograph with the pool footprint shown with stakes and a tape might be good, if the pool doesn't look too big.

In the second part of your presentation, you would probably describe how the new zoning to the larger lot requirements has foreclosed the construction of your pool. You'll also want to discuss other pools in that zone and the prior zone, and perhaps show photographs of other installations. As part of your preparation for the presentation, it might be a good idea for you to drive around and take a quick look from the street at the houses owned by the board members to see if any of them have an above-ground pool, and to determine if any of them are in the same zoning district that you are. "Ms. Perry, I know that you live up on Overlook Drive, and you probably know better than some what the situation is like on our property because your lot is also in the quarter-acre zone and was built at about the same time as ours. I understand that you have an above-ground pool in your backyard, fortunately installed before the change in zoning. I hope you find it all works just fine for you and the neighbors." You have to be careful about going too far, because some board members might think you have them under investigation, but in a small town, where you may know people and have reason to know about their properties, this can be highly effective and can turn that board member into one of your supporters.

The last part of your argument, set out on one page, would be to directly address the "practical difficulty and unnecessary hardship" test or whatever test applies in your state and under your regulations. You need to provide the board with a shorthand description of how that test is met, so that when they go to vote on your matter, they can incorporate your points in their findings and motion.

This might also be a good point at which to list a few similar variances that the board has granted that you discovered during your preparation work in reviewing prior applications. Listing the similar variances will help refresh the memories of the board members and provide them with analogies in support of your variance.

This is the time to think about who might accompany you to the presentation and speak on your behalf. In the above-ground pool case, it would be a good idea to have your spouse and your two daughters present and have them make a short statement, perhaps after your neighbors speak on your behalf. If one of them just raises her hand, apparently spontaneously, after the neighbors have spoken and says when acknowledged by the board: "I'm Milly. This is Jenny. We are here with our father. We just want to tell you that we would really like to have this pool, and that we think it would work well in our yard and fit in fine in our neighborhood. As my dad said, many other folks in our neighborhood have similar pools, and a couple of our good friends up the hill have them. We would like to have our own and be able to invite friends over to our house sometimes."

After your short presentation, it is likely that the board members will ask any questions that they have. You should try to think what those questions might be and have some answers ready. "Have you ever discussed these plans with your neighbors?" "Yes, and a couple of them are here tonight. I can tell you that none of the abutters on either side or behind have any objections. I can also tell you that no one else in the neighborhood has any objections to this variance. In fact, here's a letter that I sent around and the list of people I sent it to. No notice is required by the regulations, but I thought it was something I should do as a good neighbor." This is a dynamite response to this type of question. And if they don't ask, you can always put the letter and list in after your neighbors have spoken.

As for your supportive neighbors, you want to discuss the hearing with them in advance and have them prepared to give a very short statement identifying who they are, where they live, and where their property is in relation to yours. They can say that they have reviewed the plans with you and they support your variance. That's all you need.

The biggest problem with getting your neighbors and friends to speak in support is simply getting them there. Often, either they are too busy or they simply don't like to speak publicly. If it is clear that supporters are not going to be able to appear on your behalf, at the very least you want a letter from them sent to the board and mailed in advance. You need to have a copy, and you need to ask if the board has received it. If the board hasn't received it, you put your copy into the record.

The best thing to do with regard to supporters is to have them ride with you, so that you can be sure they get there. In some of our larger cases, where we reach out to the neighborhood in a comprehensive and organized way, we actually have a driver and car available to take people, especially the elderly, to the hearing, just to make sure that they are coming and that they get there. You'll also want to call your neighbors a couple of days before, and maybe even check in with them the evening of the hearing to make sure that they will come and support you. It is difficult to overstate the importance of having supporters physically there for you, regardless of the type of zoning application. It does take some work on your part, and maybe a little cajoling.

Believe it or not, the preparation for a major shopping center development or a residential development with hundreds of units is the same as that for a variance for an above-ground pool in your backyard—it is just that everything is bigger and more elaborate.

For larger developments, your outline might run two or three pages, but it should not be longer than that. Each part of the outline will identify the name of the speaker and her affiliation in short-hand form: "Georgina Jones, P.E., Jones & Joseph Engineers." The outline will describe what the speaker is going to say: "description of site, development plan, utilities, storm-water management, traffic." Occasionally, but not often, we list in the handout how many minutes will be devoted to each part of the presentation. We certainly know at the outset how long the total presentation will be, and we tell that to the board. We caution the board members that the time given assumes that the presentation is uninterrupted and that if there are questions, it will be longer. We leave it to the board to decide whether to ask questions during the presentation or to hold them until the end (I try to discourage interruptions, however, at least subtly), but once the board members start asking questions, the schedule is out the window.

Following the outline is a list of speakers and detailed contact information, including full company names, addresses, telephone numbers, and electronic mail and Web site addresses. The reason for this is that when there are half a dozen or more experts, most people can't keep track of who they are and what company they are affiliated with. This list provides some reinforcement for the board.

It is often useful to include a summary of important facts. This should not take more than one page and should include information about the site's current use, dimensions, and characteristics, such as wetlands, and the topography. It also includes statistics about the proposed development, including lot coverage, building dimensions, parking, total floor area, setbacks, and the number of employees. The idea is to put a single sheet with the most important facts related to the zoning proposal in the hands of each board member that can be referred to throughout the proceedings and deliberations. It also is most helpful to the presenters to have those facts and figures at hand. It can save some embarrassment: "So, what is the percentage of your lot coverage?" "I don't know offhand, I'll have to look at the plans. I think it is on the summary table on sheet 14 of 27, but let me check my plan set."

You may want to include a single small representation of the project site as it is proposed to be developed. Each board member may have a plan set, but usually these are too big to roll out.

For a large, complex project, the handout with the presentation outline may be many pages long and bound. The objective is for the board members to have a ready reference that includes virtually everything they need to know about the project team and the proposal. The actual application for a large development project may be several large binders and over 100 sheets of plans. No board member is going to be able to dig through those quickly to get essential information for a question or comment during a hearing.

Don't forget your Web site. If you put up the detailed information on your Web site, remembering that you don't want to aid and abet your adversaries at the same time, the information will be readily accessible to the board members between sessions of the public hearing and between the close of the public hearing and the time when they vote. You can make reference to your Web site in your handout and direct people there.

Orchestrating the presentation of a large project can be complex. I have been involved in some large projects where the presentation, before questions and comments by the board and before any of the opposition, consumed two full evenings. This is not desirable, but some projects can be so big and so complicated that when there is likely to be an appeal in a state in which the appeal is based solely on the record prepared during the zoning hearings, you need to have that much testimony in order to create an adequate record.

Generally, even for large projects, I think it is possible to do a good presentation in not more than an hour and a half. This takes great discipline and preparation, but if your written submission with your application and the additional written submissions that you present at the time of the hearing are sufficient, the oral presentation can be kept short. With a large project, you reasonably can expect that the staff is thoroughly familiar with the project and that the board members have received enough material in advance that you can condense your presentation.

Limiting the number of speakers can help. It is not always necessary, for example, to put on the architect and the landscape architect, if you already have an engineer presenting. Your list of speakers will include a list of additional team members who are present and available to answer questions. Your engineer, in describing the project, can identify the architect and landscape architect, who will be available to answer specific questions about those details of the plan. The engineer can briefly present the architecture and landscape architecture.

Likewise, if you have a market study, and your architect is already up there, she can summarize the results of the market study in the context of the architectural solution and leave the detailed questions to the market analyst, who is there and available. You don't get extra points for putting up lots of expensive consultants. You do get credit for succinct presentations that focus on the most important facts and issues.

Your traffic engineer is likely to have to present regardless, because traffic in most projects is that important. Traffic engineers love their subject, and, if you let them, they will go on for an hour (or more!). Traffic engineering is also (my apology to all my traffic engineering friends) among the more boring subjects, except when it comes down to laying out the solutions to traffic problems.

I have one traffic engineering consultant who is so boring that when planners are giving me a hard time, I have threatened to put on that traffic engineer for three hours straight. This is a winning strategy.

Good graphics can help here. If the traffic engineer shows an overall plan of the trip generation and distribution, noting only the few numbers that are absolutely essential, and then goes right to the solutions, this will make for a much quicker and more interesting presentation.

Orchestration also requires knowing in what order the speakers will present. Who will start? As the lawyer for a project, I usually go first, but I limit myself to a few minutes, because practically no one is interested in hearing from a lawyer. You might have the developer start the presentation and introduce the team. With the initial handout, we often include all of the curriculum vitae, so we do not need to qualify our experts orally during a presentation. In addition to the curriculum vitae, it might be useful to have a short narrative biography for each, which is more readable.

I prefer to have each speaker pass the baton to the next speaker without intervention. This is not a variety show where you need a master of ceremonies: "And now, I have for you straight from Cleveland, one of the country's absolutely best traffic engineers . . ." Instead, after the engineer presents the site, she may say simply: "I am going to pause my presentation at this point and have our environmentalist, Betsy Boggs, tell you about the wetlands on the site and how we restricted this development to protect them, then I'll be back to tell you about some of the engineering details of the project." I prefer this approach because it goes more smoothly, and it sends a couple of other messages. One is that the consultants are all so capable that they could run the show themselves—they don't need their developer client or the lawyer to tell them when to get up and when to sit down. The other message is that these consultants obviously have worked together as a team and have integrated their approaches.

A logical sequence is to have the developer or the developer's lawyer start the presentation, giving the handout and telling the board how long the presentation will take. Then the engineer presents the background of the site, followed by the environmental professional, who discusses constraints on site development. The engineer or perhaps the architect might follow and present the project. The traffic engineer makes a presentation, and then, for a bang-up ending (half facetiously), the developer or the lawyer gives a brief summary, aided by a chart or part of the handout, showing full compliance with the zoning and asking for favorable consideration of the application. You want a good speaker at the end, and you want to try to end on an upbeat note. If you are going to offer to set aside some open space, make a contribution to a housing trust fund, or provide a site for a new fire station or school, this is something you may wish to offer at the end. If you have a weak or boring presenter, you may want to sandwich that person between two good presenters.

There is no magic and no ironclad rule with regard to the order of presentation. It should make logical sense, so with most zoning campaigns, it starts with a description of what you have, then moves to the constraints on development, which, more often than not, are largely environmental and physical (like steep slopes and shallow depth to bedrock), but could include zoning. The next step is to talk about the project itself at the macro level of basic site design, gilded with architecture and landscaping. What follows next in most, but not all, zoning campaigns is a discussion of how you will mitigate the adverse impacts, which are traffic and maybe storm-water runoff. Finally, you end with a short representation that the project is in full compliance with all federal, state, and local laws and in some measure is far better than what the law requires.

With a bigger, more complex development, you might throw in a variety of other experts, including a noise consultant, market analyst, fiscal impact economist, real estate appraiser, air quality engineer, herpetologist if you have vernal pools, hydrologist, historic preservation consultant, archaeologist—why, there is an expert for just about everything.

Rehearse, and Then Rehearse Some More

All of the scripting and orchestrating you do is going to be worth nothing if your troops don't follow the script. They will not follow the script unless you rehearse.

I have seen or had reported to me just about every disaster that can occur in a public hearing. Nearly all of them happened because people didn't rehearse. I learned the hard way early in my career that I even had to pay attention to how people might dress. I had one traffic engineer many years ago, a very nice older fellow, who showed up one night at a hearing in bright plaid pants. More attention was given to his pants than to his presentation (maybe for the better, now that I think of it). He became known as "dead men don't wear plaid," and thereafter I would always double-check with him before the hearing to make sure that he was dressed a little more conservatively. I had another engineer who insisted on wearing the same pair of beat-up cowboy boots to hearings.

It is not really anyone's job to tell a professional how she should dress, but when it may reflect adversely on your team's presentation, it may be appropriate in talking about the hearing to at least mention that the particular board or commission might be influenced or distracted by not only our preparation, but our appearance, and that although "business casual" is appropriate dress, we need to present a truly professional appearance. A gentle touch can usually bring results.

If we go out to dinner before a hearing, by the way, no one drinks. It is hard enough to put on a good presentation without a couple of drinks under your belt. I did have one consultant, who had a drinking problem, show up at a hearing with alcohol on his breath. After the hearing, I took him aside and told him point-blank that if he ever again came to a hearing where I was the lawyer and he smelled of alcohol, he would never work on another job with me. This is a zero-tolerance issue. A slip of the lip can cost millions of dollars.

Two or three weeks before the hearing, you should get your consultants together and have them go over the presentation outline, allocating time to each speaker and dividing up the responsibilities for covering different portions of the presentation. Good professionals are flexible when it comes to the time they spend on their presentations, and you generally will find that they can shift time around to meet each other's needs. They can also work under a time limit, if they know what it is and they agree to control the scope of their presentation. They may advise you that you need to expand the length of time for the presentation, add or remove a speaker, or move parts of the presentation from one speaker to another. This is where a team effort is needed.

In most cases, you do not want your presenters to read from a script. You will get the best result if they prepare an outline or script their remarks and then present from a highlighted version. The presenter has to work with whatever is most comfortable. I've seen some people do great presentations with no notes, and I have seen others read verbatim in a natural voice. Then again, I've seen completely garbled presentations by people who were unprepared and had no notes, and I saw one lawyer fall asleep during his hearing because one of his experts was so boring. The poor fellow actually did fall fast asleep in the middle of his own hearing. I'm not sure what woke him up, but he came to in time to finish the hearing. He later became a judge. Go figure.

At least a few days before the hearing, you should have a full-blown dress rehearsal. Your presenters should know that it is going to be conducted just like the public hearing. They should bring all of their displays and have their remarks ready to go. The dress rehearsal goes forward with no interruptions, just exactly as it would at the actual the hearing. Everyone keeps notes on everyone else's presentations, and a critique follows. If necessary, you can repeat the presentation from start to finish. In most cases, it will be close enough to the mark on the first run to save having a second run.

By the rehearsal day, you should know what room you are going to be in, and your exhibits will be ready for that setting. If you are working from panels, either the presenter will be on the side of the room or you will have an assistant with identical panels facing the audience and silently indicating what the presenter is pointing out to the board, panel after panel, so that the audience is treated with respect and the board will not have concerns about the public's participation in the hearing.

In some cases, we have used video cameras to project the presentation to monitors around the room. We've also used monitors for PowerPoint presentations. In one instance, we used two different slide projectors, one facing toward the rear of the room that the board could watch and another facing toward the front of the room that the public could watch. It is not difficult or expensive to make these dual displays, it just takes some planning.

Even for smaller applications, the dress rehearsal can greatly increase the effectiveness of your presentation and save you from disaster. I know of a zoning application in which a traffic engineer was testifying on the impact of a moderate-sized residential development on the main street in town, which was also a state highway. There was enough traffic generation that the development had small measurable impacts on a few intersections some distance away. The traffic engineer was not well prepared, and the lawyer running the hearing did not stop his testimony. It went like this: "So, Mr. Traffic Engineer," asked a commissioner, "I guess if the traffic will go through this intersection and go on down the street here, and go a half a mile to this other intersection, there will be some impact, correct?" "Yes." "And some cars will go through the next intersection, will they not?" "Yes, I guess you could say that." "And so if they go on up over the hill, some will eventually pass through this intersection, right?" "Yes." At this point, the traffic engineer had already lost his footing on what we call a "slippery slope" line of questioning from which there is no recovery. In the end, the traffic engineer had admitted on the record that the traffic from this development would be felt at intersections six miles away in the next town. Not good.

Rehearsing doesn't just mean rehearsing the direct testimony during the hearing and the presentation of demonstrative evidence in the form of pictures and plans and even materials that may be part of the building, it also means being ready for every kind of dumb (and smart) question that might be thrown at you.

We test both the strength of the presentations and the ability to field questions by enlisting people who are not lawyers and who have no knowledge of the application (our secretaries and other staff) as "board" members for the dress rehearsal. We let them ask their own questions, and we also give them a list of questions to ask after the presentations. Most of the questions are ones that we have worked up with the consultants. Some are out of left field.

We also have some people role-play as opposition types. They may even put on their own rebuttal testimony to test how your experts respond. At the very least, they are there to ask tough questions and to help train your presenters to respond in a professional and civil manner to even the most outrageous attacks on the project personally and professionally.

After the presentation, the "board" starts peppering the consultants with questions. The consultants are challenged to answer directly and succinctly, and, importantly, not to stray from their fields of expertise. There's nothing better when you are on the other side to hear someone like a traffic engineer say: "I understand your question, but I'm not a wetlands scientist. Let me try to answer it as best I can anyway." Experts should not wander from their field under any conditions, even in friendly, informal proceedings when they really want to be helpful.

If they feel uncomfortable with a question, a simple pause in answering is usually a sufficient signal to us to intervene on their behalf and try to direct the question to someone else or get the question recast into one that they can handle. Questions that are impossible to answer are going to either go unanswered or be deferred to a continued hearing. You can politely reject scandalous and irrelevant questions.

Finally, if you still suspect after the dress rehearsal that you may have a weak link in your chain of presenters, you should not be reluctant to work with that consultant one-on-one. You can give him a call after the rehearsal and ask to meet at his office to go over his testimony one more time.

Practice makes perfect. My children will roll their eyes at this aphorism, as they hear it from me all the time. I have never seen anyone who was overprepared for a hearing, although some have spent too much time rehearsing presentations based on too little content. A room full of experts and the developer for an afternoon can cost $5,000 or more, but if it saves an extra night of a continued hearing or means the approval of a close zoning application, it is worth every penny of it.

Rehearse, and Then Rehearse Some More

Whenever I think about getting ready for the hearing, I think of that wonderful little movie *Big Night* (1996), directed by Stanley Tucci and starring Tony Shalhoub and Stanley Tucci. Shalhoub and Tucci play two brothers, Primo and Secondo. They have a chance to save their failing restaurant when a friend says he thinks he can get the jazz musician Louis Prima and his band to have dinner at the restaurant. The movie takes place in one day and one night, and is all about the preparations for the dinner. Primo is a great chef, totally dedicated, and he and his brother make an extraordinary effort to prepare the perfect meal. The great meal and a great zoning hearing both take skillful preparation and hard work. Bon appetit!

Making the Presentation

Making the presentation is the extreme event of most zoning campaigns.

It is inevitably both the best of times and the worst of times. For some people (the large majority of people who feel great anxiety when it comes to public speaking), it is traumatic. I read of a survey, unbelievable in my view, that showed that a large number of people feared having to give a public speech more than they feared death. Most people are very uncomfortable when it comes to giving public presentations.

For other people, the hearing is simply fun. The process is dynamic and exciting. Some participants will find the hearing to be a calming and culminating experience, as they bring forward all of their preparation and watch their plan gain acceptance or their opposition succeed. There are others who will see their plans, hopes, and dreams come apart as their zoning campaign goes down to defeat during the hearing.

Once again, it is preparation that is the key to success. It starts with the reconnaissance of the room and understanding exactly how you will make your presentation in terms of offering your exhibits and testimony to the board and to the public. You will have your script in hand, your outlines and supplemental materials ready to present to the board (with sufficient copies for members of the audience who may want one), and your witnesses primed and ready to go.

The zoning hearing is not a court proceeding. The board members are not judges, although they will be judging your application. They are your friends and neighbors who sit on the board, and they are much like you. Treat them with respect, but don't be unduly obsequious. If a member of the board is a good friend of yours, don't make a show of that friendship: "Hey, Bobby, good to see you. Great time at the golf tournament last weekend, wasn't it? Remember, you still owe me 10 bucks for our little wager on the 12th hole . . ." Oh, sure, you just showed everybody that you are a somebody and that you know one of the key people on the board, but you have also put your friend Bobby in a bad position. He may have to recuse himself because he is such a good friend of yours (probably not, unless the friendship goes beyond being golfing buddies), and at a minimum he will have to back off from providing active support of your project because of the appearance that his support would give.

When you speak, you should do so clearly with a strong voice to show that you have confidence in what you're saying, whether you are presenting an application of your own or opposing someone else's plans. You are not, however, Winston Churchill giving a wartime speech. Stirring oratory is seldom appropriate in a zoning hearing. Board members have heard all manner of impassioned speeches, and they are little moved by them in most cases.

This is an intimate setting, and you are usually just a few feet from the board members and the audience. It is more comfortable for them, and for you, if you make eye contact, going from one person on the board to another as you speak, and looking at the audience when you are emphasizing points for them. While you're not there to entertain people, you are likely to find it more comfortable if you are yourself, smiling when appropriate and perhaps even making a self-effacing comment: "It's a good thing I'm a teacher at the junior high school, because as you can see from my sketch plan, I don't have much of a future as an engineer. But I wanted to show you in the best way I could how this above-ground pool will work out in our backyard." What you have done with these two short sentences is explain where this crude sketch came from, that you are a dedicated public servant with limited means (something that is totally irrelevant to the proceeding, but helpful to you to have the board know), and that your principal objective is to elucidate the facts to help the board make the best decision it can.

A self-effacing comment is different from a string of apologies: "I'm sorry this preparation is so crude. I just couldn't spend the money on an engineer, and I really didn't have time to get one before I came here." Excuses and apologies will not get you anywhere.

Here is how a factory owner seeking expansion of his manufacturing facility might connect with the board: "I've been in the business of manufacturing widgets for four decades, as were my father and grandfather before me. Zoning is certainly not my business, but I'm here tonight standing before you—and I must say, I'm not very comfortable getting up here—asking that you assist me in expanding our business by approving our proposed amendments and the development agreement. I love the widget business. I get up every morning looking forward to getting out on the factory floor. I want to continue this business for my children and grandchildren, keep our local citizens employed in this important industry, and expand opportunities for additional workers, right here in my hometown."

What a great message. Here is the "hands-on" company president who, like most people, really doesn't like public speaking, but who is willing to suffer that anxiety on behalf of his employees in the community, standing before you practically hat in hand, asking you to work with him to make this possible. Notice that there is no whining: "I shouldn't have to go through this to make use of my own property." Notice also that there are no threats: "If I don't get the zoning expansion, you should know we will not be able to expand our employment and I may have to lay people off." It is almost always better to stick to the positive, personal message with outwardly directed benefits. If this factory owner can get what he wants from zoning, he will have created new value on the site at practically no cost. It will be as if the board has manufactured some new land, just as he builds widgets.

Some people present their applications as if they were playing a round of golf or working with a group of volunteers in the church garden: "Hey, okay, I really got a lot of plans here. I spent a lot of time on these. Hey, these engineers really know how to use a lot of paper, don't they? I don't know what all these squiggly lines mean." These loquacious types interject meaningless banter all along the way in order to keep the conversation going. Please don't do this. It is better to stop and have some dead air while you gather your thoughts than to throw in fillers the way you might do in a completely casual setting. These asides only waste time and show nervousness on your part or a lack of confidence in your application.

All of your rehearsal will pay off for you now. You know what you're going to say, practically word for word, and how long it will take. If your presentation is interrupted by a tough question, you will have already anticipated that question and have an answer ready. "Are your neighbors going to be able to see this pool?" "Yes, they will. I did some sketches of what part of the above-ground pool they will be able to see from their houses. I put up stakes at each corner where the above-ground pool would be, connected them with yellow plastic tape, and took photographs so you can see how the pool would fit in the yard. Here are the views from the three surrounding properties and my sketches. I also discussed this with my three neighbors, and two of them are here tonight and will speak later."

You will make mistakes. I have made every mistake in the book and many more. Perhaps my next book should be *Dwight's Most Famous Mistakes at Zoning Hearings*. I will not embarrass myself by regaling you with the worst of these mistakes, but let me give you just two examples and tell you how I handled them. They may be instructive when you inevitably make mistakes.

I was representing a client named Harboredge, and the abutting development opposing our project was called Harborside. I stood up at the beginning of the hearing and said, "Ladies and Gentlemen, my name is Dwight Merriam. I'm a lawyer at Robinson & Cole, and I represent Harborside condominiums." Eyes widened and a few giggles leaked out. This was a small town where I had been involved in several land-use matters, some of them quite controversial. I had a good relationship with the board and the townspeople. I stopped. I smiled and said: "For years, I have worried about making that mistake, and now I'm done with it. We should never let neighbors opposing each other have similar names." Everyone smiled, and we went on with the hearing.

Another time, after several grueling days of work (including many hours of dictation) followed by long hearings at night, I appeared in front of a local board exhausted, but ready to do my job. Sometimes—not a good habit, I assure you—I make my final mental organization for the hearing as I begin with my standard opening remarks, which is what I did this evening, with one dumb mistake: "Good evening, Ladies and Gentlemen period." Yes, I actually put the word *period* in at the end of this opening statement of my presentation, just as if I were still attached to the dictating machine in my office. I heard the word *period* as it came out of my mouth and realized what I was doing, but too late to suck the word back into my throat.

Some people might have stopped at that point and said: "Oh my goodness, I am so sorry. I am, I was . . . [stammer, stammer] I was really thinking ahead about what I had to say tonight and I'm kind of tired . . . we've been very busy this week, and so you can understand . . ." Forget about it. This doesn't help. It just highlights your mistake. Instead, I did what I sometimes do with a minor mistake at a hearing; I just went on as if it had never happened. I noticed a couple of board members look at me for a moment and then look at each other and sort of shrug their shoulders. I imagine that most of them were not sure what I had said and could care less anyway. Look, most people don't hear half of your mistakes, and the remainder generally could care less.

Of course, some mistakes are doozies. A lawyer friend of mine in another firm is still talked about today, many years later, for something he said during a zoning hearing. He was discussing the flora and fauna to be found in a meadow on the site, and in that part of the presentation, he had intended to talk about the various kinds of "organisms" found to use the area. "Yes," he said, "our consultants have been down there in the meadow on numerous occasions, and I can tell you there are many orgasms there." Everyone had a good laugh, and the hearing continued.

If you make a misstatement and realize it later on during the hearing, the best thing to do is fix it on the record, even though you may be embarrassed by it: "I should point out, as my engineer did during the break, that the total area of wetlands is 20 acres, not 12, as I said during my introductory remarks."

One of the most pleasurable aspects of zoning is that it is all about people. People make mistakes, and you will, too. Grin and bear it.

Think about how you appear while you are sitting in the audience in front of the board. The board members can see you just as easily as you can see them. If there are matters ahead of you on the agenda and you are waiting your turn, be sure to show respect for the board and the audience, which may include both supporters and objectors, by not talking with other people or otherwise creating a disturbance. If you need to go through your file one more time or have a conversation with someone on your team, quietly pick up and leave the room.

Often, the doors to the hearing room are left open so that the public can come and go. I have encountered many embarrassing situations where those of us in the room could overhear conversations in the hallway. Take your conversation down the hall and away from the hearing room, so that you will not be accidentally overheard.

And speaking of being overheard, you need to remember that people within earshot in the room and outside in the hallway are not necessarily friendly to your cause. Just because you do not recognize somebody or she appears to be there for some other purpose, that does not mean it is safe to have a confidential conversation around her.

During many hearings that run on for an hour or more, there will be ups and downs. Sometimes you think you have the decision in the bag, and other times you can only imagine the inevitable denial. If you're on the opposition side, you may believe you have scored a direct hit against the enemy. Never, never (did I say "never"? I mean it) show your emotion until the final decision is voted on, and probably not even then.

While some people who think they are winning during a hearing do not necessarily go so far as to give their compatriots a high-five, even a nudge, a smile, or an appreciative side remark ("oh, yes!") will be seen as gloating. The board has the power to punish you for that by making the rest of the hearing difficult or perhaps even rejecting your position, whether it is for or against a project.

Even unconsciously, you may turn the board against you. Just pretend that you are a poker player bluffing yourself out of a bad hand or about to up the ante while holding a straight flush. Give nothing away with your demeanor. Do not embarrass the board, your opponents, or yourself by reacting during the process.

Of course, emotion has its place during the hearing. If someone attacks you personally and says something hurtful, it is entirely appropriate for you to reflect on that, at least in passing: "I'm sorry that Mrs. Jones felt it was important to comment on the unpopular decision I had to make as chair of the Parks and Recreation Commission. I find it hurtful, but it is not relevant to this proceeding, and I intend to focus strictly on this application."

One of the biggest challenges of managing the public hearing presentation, especially in the majority of states where judicial appeals are on the record, is ensuring that the record is complete and accurate. While we cover litigation in Chapter 16, let's do the short version here. There are two types of appeals. One of them is a de novo appeal, which means that the trial court essentially hears the matter all over again, just as it was presented at the local level. In the de novo appeal states, sometimes the presentation at the local level is almost ceremonial when an appeal appears inevitable.

In other states, the appeals are on the record, which means that all the court has is what it finds in the record—in the transcript of the hearing and the exhibits that have been made part of the record. The "trial" in the record appeal states is merely an argument by the two lawyers concerning the facts and the law, with little or no testimony. There is no parade of expert witnesses. The court simply reads the testimony from the local administrative proceedings. I once had an appeal in a significant case involving a 400-unit expansion of a large residential condominium project in which the opposing counsel and I agreed to the judge's request that he "take it on the papers." There was no argument in court, and the "trial" was over in five minutes. The judge retired to his chambers and over the next several weeks pored over the voluminous record before rendering his decision.

I have worked mostly in record appeal states, and when I speak or hear others speak at a public hearing, I actually imagine that we are speaking to the judge directly, because ultimately we will be. The record speaks to the judge, both in the oral testimony and in the documentary exhibits. You may organize and present the record in a somewhat different light during the appeal, but the record will always be the record. It cannot be more, and it cannot be less. When you speak to the record, think of yourself as speaking to the judge.

Sometimes during a hearing, when it is necessary to take care of technicalities involving the record, I will even explain why I'm doing it: "I'm sorry to have to be as precise as I am regarding what exhibits are in and what exhibits are out, but, regrettably, sometimes these zoning cases end up in front of a judge, and I want to make sure that we are clear as to what is in this record."

In a record appeal case, you may have some problems preparing a good record that will be clear to the judge, especially when there is informal oral testimony. Imagine that you are part of a neighborhood group opposing a project, and you have engaged a professional engineer to review the storm-water management plan. You are concerned about flooding on the development site and the impacts off-site in your neighborhood.

Your engineer has gone over the development plans in detail and prepared a report. He is now speaking as a rebuttal witness at the public hearing. His testimony is compelling, and he clearly has the attention of the board. The developer's engineer is literally wriggling in his seat as your engineer rips up his design. Unfortunately, even though you convince the board to deny the application because of the failure of the developer to properly manage storm water on- and off-site, the developer appeals.

The record that goes up on appeal is not all that helpful to the judge because your engineer's testimony as transcribed reads: "Yes, over here, down where this part of the stream goes; no, not downstream, over here; you'll see that the elevation up at this point is not as it should be. I think if you go down here and if the storm water were to be rerouted around to the basin and on through here, changing this elevation from 13.0 to 16.7, that might work. But that's not all, really over here on the other sheet of the plans, which here I can get out for you. Here it is. This is the real problem. I never would have designed this part of the watershed retention basin as you see it here."

This testimony is just about useless. You cannot argue the facts in a brief. You cannot reconcile this oral testimony with the plans presented by the developer's engineer. Unless your engineer has presented a detailed written report, you have virtually no evidence for your position. How do you keep this from happening, not only with your engineer, but with your own testimony?

When you do your dress rehearsal, think of the words that are being spoken as if they were being typed on a page and consider what the transcript will look like to the judge. If there are critical points of reference to maps and plans, photographs, and the like, you need to train your speakers (and yourself!) to "speak to the record."

Please, you do not need to say, as so many people do, "for the record." Everything you say during the hearing is for the record. You never need to say that something is for the record. If you say "for the record" during a hearing where I'm present, I will apologize now for grunting. I can't help it when somebody says those words.

Instead, your engineer, if properly trained during the rehearsal, might have given his testimony this way: "I am referring now to sheet two of three of the plan set, which is part of the application, and I would like to point out to you that at this location near catch basin 14-2, about ten feet north of it—may I circle it in red? Thank you. I am now circling it in red. This area is where the plan is really deficient. Now look up here to watershed "2" on the same sheet two of three of the plans, just northwest of the intersection of the proposed Mulberry Street and Elm Lane. There is a retention basin shown on the plan here as being approximately 0.72 acres in area. The elevation as shown on this plan, as you can see just a couple of feet west of manhole 16, is indicated as 13.0 feet. To carry the amount of storm water that is necessary to protect this property and the abutting property to the north, the elevation for the 100-year flood should be 16.7 feet at this location."

Now, the judge has something she can sink her teeth into because she knows exactly what your engineer is talking about. The engineer's testimony is now firmly grounded at fixed locations on identified plans. This transcript will give you something precise to argue about during the trial, if that becomes necessary. You could even put up the plan set during the argument in court, replicate the engineer's critical testimony, and explain to the court why the record supports the board's decision to deny the application.

What happens if your engineer or one of your spirited neighbors who has no training in the business of making good zoning presentations goes off on a long explanation where you can't even tell what map or plan she is referring to? You can interject a little "midcourse correction" in an informal and casual way: "I might just note that Mrs. Jones is referring to the traffic management plan that Mr. Buchsbaum put up during his testimony. It is entitled 'Traffic Management Plan for Mountainside Condominiums.' Importantly, the accident history she mentioned was, as she pointed out on the plan, at the intersection of Swamp Hollow and Shady Glen Roads." Now, you have anchored Mrs. Jones's testimony to a definite location on a specific plan.

Finally, when something interesting happens during the hearing that might make a difference in the outcome because it is symbolic, you may want to weave that into your presentation. I had a case during my first year of practice (1979!) in which a board member who had a conflict of interest recused himself from participating in the proceeding. He sat in the back of the room, but when the chairman of the board asked for anybody who wanted to speak in favor of the application (I was representing a neighborhood group opposing it), the recused board member trotted up to the front of the room and took a position of prominence at the podium to speak. The board's lawyer told the chairman that the recused board member could not speak. The chairman told the recused board member that he could not speak. The recused board member returned to his seat at the back of the room.

This was a highly contentious proceeding, and I certainly wanted to make a point then, and for the record, of what this recused board member had done, so I stood up and said: "May the record reflect that Mr. Recused Member, when the chairman asked for anyone who wanted to speak in favor of the application, left his seat in the back row of this hearing room and walked the full length of the hearing room, approximately 100 feet, in full view of everyone, up to the podium where all speakers have addressed the board and the audience, and took a position there ready to speak before he was interrupted by the chairman. I consider this to have been a statement by the recused board member that he supported the application." The "may the record reflect" was the rare exception to the usual rule that you should never say, "This is for the record." I was stirring the pot.

If you want to do the same thing in a more subtle and informal manner, the next time you have occasion to speak, you might say in passing: "While we concur that Mr. Recused Member shouldn't be participating, I think it's unfortunate that the chairman had to direct Mr. Recused Member not to speak after he walked up to the podium from the back of the room where he was seated." You do not need to say that the Recused Member's walking to the front was in response to the chairman's asking for comments in favor of the application, because the record as transcribed will show that the next statement on the record after the chairman asked for speakers in favor was the chairman telling the recused member that he would not be allowed to speak.

What I wanted in the record was that he took a position of prominence in the front of the room. I could use that to argue that it was a statement in favor of the project that might be used to reverse the entire proceeding if the outcome was not in our favor. It is one of those procedural due process problems that can defeat a vote and get you back to a new hearing.

Actually, "may the record reflect" is a little different from "for the record," because it is used to put into the record something that would not be self-evident from the transcript or documents. For example, although it is never proper for a board to poll the audience as to how it should vote, it might be useful for you to get into the record something about the number of people in attendance and their apparent support or opposition: "I think it is important to note that this is such an important matter that in this town of just 1,200 people, we have about 400 people in the room tonight, and I think you'll agree with me that about two thirds of those people are wearing buttons that say: 'shelter the homeless.' The people of this town want you to approve this proposed shelter."

Don't hold back in being creative in making the record. Twenty years ago, I represented a neighborhood group that wanted to pre- serve a large bluff overlooking the ocean. To get a sense of the site, one of the neighbors drove her car with an infant on her lap along the road surrounding the site. It was a home movie, if there ever was one, but it was good evidence.

In a case where I was trying to get a marina approved, I once saw a too-earnest opponent plunk down on the hearing examiner's table a neatly cut one-foot-square section of *Spartina alternaflora* marsh grass, with roots and soil. It was dramatic, but keeping it in the record was not practical.

I was representing a gravel-mining operation in a small town of a few thousand people. The neighbors did not want the noise of the excavation equipment. During a warm-weather hearing with all the windows open, the neighbors were offering their testimony opposing expansion of the gravel mine, making the argument that the OSHA-required backing signals disturbed them. Right on cue, a large pickup truck started backing up to an open window, its backing alarm beeping away. A nice demonstration, but a little difficult to get into the record in a form that a judge could review later.

The best evidence does not always come from experts. Neighborhood groups can be highly effective in making and presenting their own traffic counts and reporting on accident histories. One of the best witnesses I ever had appeared in a complex case involving excavating sand and gravel from a river bottom. The state's scientists had argued that our client should not excavate as deeply as proposed because oxygen levels would be reduced and the eel fishery would suffer. Our "expert" witness was a successful commercial eel fisherman who fished this stretch of the river and airfreighted most of his catch to France. The fisherman was rough and sunburned, with gnarled hands and fingers bent by years of pulling lines. He testified that he got the most eels at the bottom of the deepest pits already dredged by our client. His testimony was devastating to the state's position, and we received our permit. The client dredged his sand and gravel, the fishermen caught eels, and the French ate them. Life was good.

Responding to Questions and Rebutting the Opposition

After your presentation, after the board has asked for any questions and people have spoken in favor of and in opposition to your proposal, you will have an opportunity to respond to unanswered questions and to rebut the opposition.

Presumably, your solid preparation will have you ready to answer just about any question. These answers should be short and direct. Your demeanor should be even-tempered. If a question comes out that you did not imagine, answer it matter-of-factly. If you are asked for information you do not have, if that information is important enough, you might ask that the hearing be continued to another night so that you can get the information and respond. Otherwise, answer as best you can, while admitting that you do not have full information. Invite a condition on the approval, if necessary.

For example, if the neighbors ask, "Can you assure me that the parking lot lights will not shine in my bedroom window?" you might explain that the lighting is designed to shine down on the lot and not onto adjoining property. You might suggest that the board condition the approval on using hooded lights that direct the light downward and away from the abutting properties, and that prior to the issuance of the certificate of occupancy for the store, the staff should approve the specifications for the parking lot lighting. This allows you to close the hearing, get your approval, and go forward with your construction while you work out the details of the parking lot lighting. It is a strong gesture of goodwill to the neighbors, and it demonstrates that you are ready, willing, and able to work for the neighborhood's benefit.

Handling the Unexpected

The unexpected happens more often than you would expect. Computers crash, overhead projectors break, the janitor fails to provide the electric power promised, and a snowstorm makes it difficult for you and your witnesses to get to the hearing on time. Be flexible. If you can't do the full "dog and pony show" that you planned, simply explain the technical difficulties and go on with the hard copies that you brought with you as backup. If the meeting is delayed because of bad weather, relax and go forward when you can. Don't feel rushed, and don't show any impatience. If going forward appears untenable, simply request that the hearing be continued to another night.

What do you do with an unruly member of the public? It is best to stop your presentation and allow the chair to handle the situation. Sometimes it may even be necessary to call in the police. I have seen that on two occasions, on one of which a member of the board was directly threatened during a hearing. If it becomes impossible to continue, recommend to the board that it suspend the hearing and continue it another night. This usually happens when the room is too small to allow all those who are interested to participate. People should never be left outside in the hall, because if they are, they will not have an adequate opportunity to see and respond to the evidence. If you cannot immediately find a larger room elsewhere and post a sign on the original room indicating where the hearing will take place, the hearing should be continued to another night when you can find a space of sufficient size.

Hearings seldom go as planned, and you may wonder whether you have everything you need in the record or whether the hearing really ought to be continued to another night. Only you can judge whether the record is sufficient to convince the board to vote for your position and, if the board goes against you, whether it is sufficient to make it possible for you to win on appeal. Some boards are intolerant of presentations that run on for several hours or even several nights. You may only harm your position by filibustering rather than closing things up. This is one of the toughest calls to make in a zoning campaign. Probably the best rule to remember is that the record does not have to be perfect, it just has to be good enough.

Whether I'm on the developer's side or with the opposition, if I think I have all the points I need in the record, and if I have a sense that the board is ready to go with our side, I generally want to close the hearing, even if the record is less than perfect. It is also difficult and expensive to bring back several consultants to a continued hearing. Most, if not all, of those consultants will need to be at a continued hearing to hear the evidence on the other side, to respond to new evidence, and to be available to answer questions. The continued hearing can be an expensive proposition.

Before the hearing is closed, you may wish to provide the board with draft findings of fact and findings of law. The findings of fact reflect the evidence that you put on during the hearing. Because you know the law and the evidence that you will put on before the hearing even starts, you can draft these findings beforehand. A finding of fact in the above-ground pool case might be: "The lot was subdivided and developed in 1962 with a single-family house when the area was zoned for quarter-acre lots." A finding of law might be: "The statutory hardship standard is met in that there are unique characteristics of the lot replicated on few other parcels."

The hearing is over, but your work continues.

PART IV

POSTHEARING FOLLOW-UP

Chapter 15

Procedural Issues and the Vote

After the hearing, it may be two weeks or even a month or two before the board votes. Sometimes, the board will vote the same night, particularly if the application is simple and straightforward, like the above-ground pool example. For most other, more complex applications, the staff and the board will need time to study the evidence and prepare findings of fact and law.

Here's a piece of advice worth 100 or 1,000 times the cost of this book. After the hearing is closed and before the vote, do not have any contact with board members regarding your application or your opposition to someone else's application. This can so taint the process that a court will readily set aside the zoning board's vote and send the case back to start all over again. I have had clients get in this jam more than once, and it has become my strictest policy to tell clients that after the hearing is over, they cannot talk to members of the board no matter what. Any critical follow-up information might be provided to the planner or other staff members, but even that can put you at risk in some states and under some conditions.

This makes sense because not everyone involved in the process is privy to those communications after the hearing. We call this ex post facto evidence—evidence received outside of the record that becomes, intended or not, part of the record and potentially influences the decision makers. It is a violation of constitutional law in that it prevents other parties to a proceeding from being able to confront and rebut the evidence. The benefits of trying to be helpful by passing on additional information after the hearing is closed are far outweighed by the costs of having a reversal of a favorable decision and being required to start all over again, with the opposition now fully educated as to your application.

In most jurisdictions, it is unlikely that you will be able to speak at all at the time of the vote. Some boards operate more informally, and you might be asked a question or two during the deliberations. You will need to make the decision on the spot as to whether it is worth the risk of being accused of giving ex post facto information, or whether the risk of rebuffing the request for information is greater. In small towns and in informal proceedings, it may be better to err on the side of providing information: "Would you be willing to do some extra plantings along the side yard if we granted your application?" It is going to be difficult to answer: "I believe that any response to that question would be evidence outside of the record in violation of the due process rights of other parties to this proceeding, so I elect not to answer your question at this time and suggest that you not ask me any further such questions."

More probably than not, your answer will be yes, which you will offer knowing that there is some risk. I do not condone your violating the due process rights of others; I'm just telling you that as a practical matter, this is the way it usually goes.

When I have been caught in that situation as a lawyer, I politely try to avoid giving an evidentiary answer: "I'm sorry, but because the hearing is over, I can't respond to any specific inquiry you may have on such conditions that you could reasonably impose on your approval." This is not an evidentiary response, but it signals the board that we are open to a condition. This is a fine line, I admit.

If you are the applicant, and things appear to have broken down completely and you see a denial coming, you may want to immediately request a withdrawal of your application before the denial. In some jurisdictions, a denial may preclude you from reapplying for some time and could be prejudicial to your other interests, whereas a withdrawal of an application may position you to address concerns expressed during the board's deliberations.

Sometimes the board may be direct about what it wants you to do: "I think we're headed towards denying your application. It is incomplete. Would you care to withdraw it before we proceed?" This is the kind of hint you ought to take, if at all possible.

Do not think that you can stay home and watch a television show while your application is being voted on simply because you know you will not have a chance to speak at that meeting. If you do not care enough about your application to go and sit in the front row and look each one of those board members in the eye while they are deliberating on your fate, then you may deserve a denial. If you are on the opposition side, you want to turn out the largest number of people you can for the deliberations and the vote to show the board that you care and that you have great staying power—and political power when election time comes.

Again, the vote is not the time to show your emotion. Regardless of the outcome, whether you win or lose, you need to stand up before you leave the room, face the chair and say, "Thank you, Madame Chair and members of the board, for your attention and consideration." You will probably be back in front of the board, perhaps even on this application, and you need to maintain and strengthen your working relationship with the board. You will do that by taking the high road every chance you get, no matter how much it hurts.

Chapter 16

After the Vote: Litigate, Reapply, or Walk Away?

No matter how the vote turns out, some member of the media—probably a cub reporter covering zoning, the board of education, the board of finance, and peewee football—will be after you in an attempt to win a Pulitzer Prize for local reporting. A short, succinct statement is the most you need. I seldom talk to the press on any matter in which I am the lawyer, before, during, or afterward. I used to talk to the press, but after many years I realized that there was very little upside and lots of downside. I ultimately concluded that it is much better to try to stay under the radar, particularly with development applications. I am most pleased with the cases in which we get through the approval process with no newspaper coverage. Many people believe that their cause may be aided by the press or like to see their names in print.

This is not to say that the media are unimportant to your zoning campaign. With some matters, it is essential to have a public relations and media consultant who can help you shape your message and get it out there. Developers and their lawyers are generally (perhaps I should say universally) not skilled at this.

This is not a time to attack the board if you do not like the outcome. You may say that you are "disappointed" or that you believe that the board may not have "fully understood" some of the issues presented, but beyond that you gain little ground by taking the offensive.

The most important step after the vote is to implement the plan that you developed at the time you put your application or opposition plan together. You drew a cascading series of critical paths showing what might happen and what your options are with each eventuality. Now you're looking at an approval, an approval with conditions, or a denial, and you need to review your plans and decide which of the alternatives you identified earlier you might pursue.

If you have lost, you always have the null alternative—the "do nothing" alternative, which is to do exactly what the name says, nothing. Let it go and go on to something else. If you need a site for a fast-food restaurant and you could not get this one approved, go find another site. If you are unable to stop a 24-hour convenience store from going into your neighborhood, go back and see what you can do to amend the zoning ordinance to keep it from happening again nearby or elsewhere in your community.

Instead of walking away, you might reapply. They turned down your apartment project this time, but perhaps if you scale it back, redesign the buildings, provide screening for the parking, and work with the local commission on aging to provide some single-room-occupancy apartments for the elderly, you can bootstrap this project into an approval. Now that you have no pending application, you might have another informal preapplication meeting with the board to discuss in detail the members' concerns as expressed during the deliberations and the vote and to test whether the board will approve something different.

Finally, if all else fails, and you have both the money and the stomach for it, you can litigate. If you are in a record appeals state, it will probably be somewhat less expensive than if you are in a de novo appeals state (but still more expensive than you can ever imagine) to take an appeal to the trial court, and from there to the appellate court level, if necessary.

At the time you conceptualized the zoning process, you were already putting together the evidence necessary to prove your case to the zoning board and to provide a powerful record that would enable you to win on appeal if you lost at the administrative level. Winning on appeal is difficult because the courts generally give great deference to local administrative decision makers. A local board or commission has to do something patently wrong before a trial court will reverse it.

Some cases are so self-evident that it is possible to predict with a high degree of certainty that a judicial appeal will succeed. A variance granted without the required finding of practical difficulty and unnecessary hardship is an easy target for an appeal. An application where the public notice was incomplete or published on the wrong date is also worthy of an appeal. Sometimes, appeals are taken more to wear down the other side than for their own merits, but it must be remembered that it is unethical and illegal to bring an action without probable cause or for an improper purpose.

In litigation generally, most cases are settled; very few cases go to trial and judgment. But, it is actually more difficult to settle zoning appeals than to settle many other types of cases, because public officials do not like to be criticized for giving in to developers or opposition groups. They would rather make their decisions and suffer court appeals and reversals than settle a case for half a loaf rather than none.

Ever the optimist, I still try to settle most cases, whether I am representing the property owner or developer, the opposition, or the government. I guess we have been able to settle only about one-fifth of our zoning cases. This lackluster record is not only because of the tendency of governments to prefer having a judge tell them what to do, but also because the cost of a record appeal might actually be competitive with the cost of a protracted process of alternative dispute resolution in a complex case.

The problem with litigation is that not only is it expensive, but it is for the most part unpredictable. I am equally as surprised by the cases I have lost as I am by the cases I have won. I have given up predicting outcomes, except in the most obvious of "slam dunk" cases, which are few and far between.

The plain fact is that we do very little litigation today compared to 20 years ago, because we spend far more time preparing prior to the hearing and getting as much right as we possibly can during the hearing in order to maximize the chances for a successful result from the board. We also prefer to reapply rather than litigate. When we do litigate, we try hard to move the parties to some type of alternative dispute resolution. To be successful in resolving these disputes, you need to leave your ego at home. Whether you are the developer, the property owner, the leader of the neighborhood group, the lawyer, or the engineer, it is never about you. It is about the land, the objectives in developing or saving it, and the zoning. You may end up looking like a chump personally and professionally, you may take hits in the press, your neighbors and your professional peers may rumormonger, but if you are truly focused on getting the best result you can from the zoning process, you will transcend all of that.

If you applied for 200 apartments, the commission granted you 175 units, and then the neighbors appealed, what are the economics of settling for 150 units and a good tax deduction for a gift of open space to a land trust, as compared with litigating 175 units and perhaps losing all of them? The calculus is not always easy, but it must be done. If there is money to be made by getting your development up and operating sooner rather than later, and if you have carrying costs for your property, then you are likely to be headed for some type of negotiated settlement.

If you are an opposition group, dare you risk having all 175 units when you could cut this project by 25 units and secure a substantial piece of open space forever through a settlement?

One thing that is certain is that the time limits for taking a zoning appeal in most states are very short. The statute of limitations may be several years in a contract case. In a personal injury case, you might have two or three years to bring suit. A zoning appeal in most states must be filed in a couple of weeks or a month. You do not have time to negotiate before taking an appeal.

When you take the appeal, it is a good idea to limit the bridges that you burn in the process. No one likes to be sued, and most people don't like to sue. If you are caught in a situation where the short statute of limitations requires you to appeal a zoning decision, and you are justifiably uncomfortable with doing that, consider saying so. I sometimes will write a letter to the board or the board's lawyer, saying that I regret having to take the appeal, but that the statute of limitations is short, and in order to protect our client's rights, I need to take the appeal. I express my hope that we will be able to work out a settlement. I usually also offer to help in any way I can in preparing a record and facilitating an economic and efficient judicial review.

We have developed a mantra that others might consider. Our objective for developers is to get them a unanimous approval with no opposition. Ending up in litigation is often, though not always, the result of something having gone wrong in the process before the board.

PART V

WINNING STRATEGIES

Chapter 17

Be Imaginative

ighly successful zoning practitioners are not linear thinkers. They don't go from A to B to C. They are synoptic thinkers—they see A, B, and C all at once, and they consider the interconnections and the opportunities for combinations and permutations.

Think about all of the different ways you can accomplish the same objective. You might amend a definition or change a regulation. You might amend a zoning map. You might add or subtract permitted uses. You might move a use from being forbidden to being allowed by some discretionary approval, such as a special permit. Instead of using zoning, you might use covenants and restrictions to achieve the degree of control you need. You might use the government's power to acquire property to achieve ultimate control. Infrastructure might be developed or denied in ways that force development in one direction or another. You might tax what you wish to discourage and provide tax credits or other financial benefits for what you want to encourage. Fast-track permitting might be available for desirable uses.

Imaginative approaches include looking at the larger landscape to reject one potential site in favor of another. From the opposition's perspective, it may be that you give up on one favored target so that can focus your limited resources on a developer or proposal where you think you will have a greater chance of success. Everyone in the zoning process has limited resources, some more limited than others. Everyone must pick and choose among several alternatives. Your challenge will be to identify the points where the use of your resources will be most efficient and effective.

As the lawyer for large-scale developers, I have often been involved in the choice of sites. Is it worth our time, effort, and money to get approval to build on this property when we might have a somewhat less desirable location where the process will be more certain and expeditious? As a member of the board of directors, and later a member of the legal advisory committee, of an environmental advocacy organization, we had very much the same discussion when it came to deciding where to use the organization's limited resources. Yes, one site might be important, but does it present issues that are of statewide importance?

Imagination in the zoning process might involve redesigning a proposal to provide a better fit with what a local board and the neighbors see as acceptable. I helped get a McDonald's approved in a town with a reputation for being exceedingly difficult. It is remarkable that this new store was finally approved, when no one else thought we could pull it off, because we put a colonial skin on the building and agreed to the board's request that we make the play space "more colonial." A two-story, glass-enclosed colonial play space—think about it.

In another case, a modest alteration of the back facade of a Home Depot carried the day, and it was approved over some opposition. While corporate retailers need to maintain their architectural identity as an important element of branding, a little flexibility can go a long way in getting an approval.

The phasing of a project can also make the difference between an approval and a denial. If a small town feels overwhelmed by the idea of 200 new units of housing, and you know, as a developer, that you are unlikely to achieve market absorption of more than 30 to 40 units per year, you can readily offer a condition that no more than 50 units will be constructed each year, stretching the construction and the impact on the community of the 200 units over a four-year period.

Rezonings

Rezonings include amendments to regulations, which can be changes to the map or to the text only.

You can sometimes get what you need through a text amendment that changes a single word or number: "Amend table 1-6, 'setbacks,' column 3, under the I-2 district to read '25.'" With this one change, you have just cut the side-yard setback requirements in the industrial zone where your factory is located from 50 feet to 25 feet. This is not to suggest that no one will notice the change; it is to point out that a single change can have large economic consequences.

A text change can add, delete, limit, or expand uses in certain districts. A use that is presently allowed only with a discretionary approval may be made as-of-right with an amendment, saving you from going through a public hearing and cutting off most, if not all, of the risk of opposition. On the other side, if you are an opposition group, you may want to move some uses from the as-of-right category into discretionary approvals.

Map amendments may require a prior change in the master plan, sometimes called the plan of development or the comprehensive plan. In some states, consistency with the plan is required, and in those states you will need to amend the plan first, before you can amend the zoning text or map. Most states do not have the consistency doctrine, and so you'll be able to amend the zoning directly.

Amending the zoning map might involve extending a district into another area. If you own a residential lot immediately adjacent to a commercial zone, you may seek to have the commercial zone extended to include your property, thereby increasing its value. A zoning amendment might move the entire area of a district into a different district, such as rezoning an area that includes not only your property but hundreds of others from a moderate-density residential district to a higher-density district.

Be wary of "spot zoning." This term is widely used, but it seldom actually determines the outcome of map amendments. The notion behind the spot-zoning doctrine is that a single property or small area should not be singled out for benefit, usually to the exclusion or detriment of others. If you own a one-acre residential lot in the middle of a one-acre district, and you seek a rezoning to commercial use so that you can put a gas station there, you are likely to be attacked as spot-zoning the property, and you will join that exclusive, small subset of cases in which the doctrine actually matters.

On the other hand, suppose you own a vacant quarter-acre residential lot immediately adjacent to an industrial district that you want to have rezoned to industrial so that you can sell it to the factory owner next door. Even though your property is quite small and even though the change will economically benefit you tremendously, this is not spot zoning in most jurisdictions.

It is not really the size of the parcel to be rezoned. Some rather large parcels have been found to be spot-zoned, and some rather small parcels of even fractions of an acre have been found not to be spot-zoned. The gist of the doctrine is that no property should be rezoned out of context with the surrounding zoning and uses.

Without a doubt, the "floating zone" is the most powerful, flexible, and creative technique for landowners and developers, for government officials, and even for those who are concerned about new developments in their community. In just about every one of the 26 years I have taught land-use law, I have included a question about floating zones in the final examination (my students who read this book, take heed).

We call it a floating zone because we imagine it floating up in the sky over the treetops above a community, ready to drift down onto a piece of land. The floating zone starts with a text amendment—no map amendment, just an amendment to the text. That text describes a potential development, usually one of a larger scale, perhaps with a mix of uses, such as residential and retail together. The text describes a minimum area for such a development, say 50 acres, although there is no magic minimum number and it could be a few acres or 100 acres or more. The text also describes where the floating zone might be located, such as within the existing multifamily zone, within a retail zone, or within a certain radius of the center of town. The text is also likely to include certain infrastructure requirements for the floating zone. It might specify the availability of public water and sewers, or location on or access to a major thoroughfare.

While floating zones are often highly flexible in that they do not mandate specific setbacks, side yards, lot coverage, open-space ratios, or even parking requirements, they will probably specify the types of uses, mix of uses, and maximum density in units per acre, square feet per acre, floor area ratio, or some other appropriate measure limiting the overall development density.

Now here is where the real power comes. You have this text, you have a site, and you have the opportunity to design a major development while giving your site planner, engineer, and architect great flexibility. Your site is of the correct size, it is in one of the listed locations, and it has all of the necessary infrastructure called for in the floating zone. However, you know that preparing detailed engineering and architectural plans for the project you want to build will cost you hundreds of thousands of dollars, and you are afraid that the project might not meet with community acceptance. You can take the same piece of land and develop an as-of-right residential subdivision, making substantially less money, but with virtually no risk.

Reading the floating-zone regulations a second time, you realize how perfect this will be for you. These floating-zone regulations do not require that you come in with detailed engineering plans or final architectural plans; instead, you start with just a concept plan showing the number of residential units, the location and size of the retail space, the road network, and generalized architectural schemes. You need to provide a narrative on the availability of water, sewers, and other utilities for the site and a preliminary traffic report. No detailed engineering! No final architectural plans! You pencil in the numbers and find that you can come in with this information for less than $50,000, a small sum compared to the potential upside of such a project.

You are also thrilled that you are no longer trapped by the usual setback and side-yard requirements, so that you can place buildings where they fit the best in this unique landscape. You can vary the parking ratios as necessary to serve the development, knowing that the parking has to work in order for your project to be marketable. Also, there is no specificity about landscaping, and you have some wonderful ideas on how you can make this particular property spectacular through landscaping.

The process for the floating zone allows you to apply for a preliminary approval of the mapping of your property under the floating-zone regulations based on the concept plan. We call this "landing" the floating zone. This is a legislative proceeding with a public hearing, just like any other zoning amendment. With this preliminary approval, you will be able to lock in the general layout, the number of residential units, the square feet and location of the retail development, and all of the basic development standards. It is just as if you had a development agreement. You do not need to "undertake substantial construction in reliance on a building permit" to vest your rights. Under the regulations, you will have a certain period of time (say, two years) to commence construction and a longer period (say, ten years) to complete it.

You also find, when you talk with your banker, that these vested rights under the conceptual plan approval are sufficient to finance all of the detailed engineering and architectural work that will need to be done in order to get to the level of construction drawings. The floating-zone regulations allow you to submit those plans in several phases. You will have outlined those phases in your original concept plan. As you come in with each small phase of buildings, you will present the site plan at a public meeting or maybe at a more formal public hearing. The zoning board will have very limited discretion at the site-plan stage, and you will be largely protected from any changes.

Try the floating zone. You will like it.

Special Permits and Conditional Uses

You will recall from Chapter 7 that special permits, special use permits, and conditional uses are all the same type of quasi-discretionary approval. It is just that different states call them by different names.

In most jurisdictions, special permits are an administrative type of approval. They are not legislative, like an amendment to the zoning regulations or a map amendment (including the floating zone), and at the other extreme, they are not quasi-judicial (or adjudicative, which is a different name for the same thing), like a zoning enforcement appeal or a variance. Special permits command that great middle ground between the largely discretionary zoning amendment and the process with little or no discretion, which includes not only the zoning enforcement review but other administrative approvals such as subdivision and site-plan review.

Given this betwixt-and-between position, special permits can provide great flexibility for new types of land uses and land uses that are not going to be allowed as of right.

Suppose you want to establish a group home for single teenage mothers. You want them to live in a typical single-family residential neighborhood, but the restrictive definition of family will not allow you to have more than four unrelated people living together.

You have determined that an economically workable arrangement is probably six young mothers or mothers-to-be and not more than two caregivers.

When you have an informal meeting with the zoning board, it is clear that the board does not want such group homes to be an as-of-right use for any house in any part of any residential district. At the same time, the board members are sympathetic to your cause and expressly recognize the need for at least one such home in your community.

The special permit is an effective way to address the zoning issue. You can draft an amendment to the regulations permitting a group home for unwed mothers operated by a nonprofit agency, with up to two caregivers and not more than six mothers and their infant children (up to one year in age). You can add additional criteria, such as requiring that there not be more than two mothers and their babies per bedroom, that the house be within walking distance of public transportation, that the house be on a lot of at least one-half acre, and that no more than four motor vehicles be parked on the property, not including guests.

You analyze these criteria, ones that you have largely created out of whole cloth in order to address what you perceive to be the concerns of the zoning board, and you find that more than half of the residential area in town still qualifies, so you are not concerned about finding a house to buy or rent somewhere.

This approach is acceptable to the zoning board, and it adopts the regulation with little opposition. The board adds an additional provision about "compatibility with surrounding properties in the neighborhood." This provision will be difficult to interpret and enforce, and in some jurisdictions it would not meet the substantive due process constitutional test because it is vague.

This compatibility provision points to one of the problems with the quasi-discretionary special-permit process. Often, the criteria intended to make sure that the use will work at the proposed site without harming the neighborhood are highly subjective. If the neighbors of your proposed group home for unwed mothers decide to oppose it, there is likely to be a highly contentious public hearing and subsequent litigation. Everyone may have his or her own idea of what "compatibility" means. This will be played out during a hearing and in court. The outcome will be unpredictable.

The challenge with special permits is to craft regulations that provide the local board with enough discretion to be able to decide, responsibly and appropriately, whether a particular use will work within a neighborhood and, at the same time, enable applicants to determine with some certainty whether their application should and will be approved.

The special permit, in most jurisdictions, can also be neatly tailored to site-specific issues through conditions imposed on the permit. With a group home for unwed mothers, a board might wish to condition the approval on the planting of a landscaped buffer along the edge of the property. It might be appropriate to require a fenced play yard. Sometimes, a time limit on the permit, so that the applicant must return to the board in a year or two or five and renew the permit, can be helpful in winning over the neighborhood. A time limit can help satisfy the board that if it approves the special permit and there are operational problems later, it will be able to terminate the special permit at the end of the period by not renewing it. The law obviously varies greatly from state to state, but it is important in some jurisdictions that the conditions be signaled in the regulation: "The special permit for a group home for unwed mothers may be conditioned on screening or buffering from surrounding properties, adequate play facilities for children, off-street parking, and time limits on the permit of not less than three years."

Finally, special permits have been in such widespread use for so long for traditional uses, such as churches, funeral homes, farm stands, day-care centers, and professional offices, that their common acceptance and familiarity make them a good candidate for new uses.

The types of special permits are limited only by your imagination. A large home-improvement center wants to have a snack bar inside its building, but restaurants are not permitted in that district. A special permit for restaurants of less than 2,000 square feet within retail uses of over 100,000 square feet would be a workable approach. An ophthalmologist wants to create a wholly owned subsidiary retail business to sell eyeglasses and wants to have it in the same building as her office, but retail uses are not allowed in the professional office district. A special permit allowing a retail operation in a medical office, if the retail operation is owned and controlled by the office tenant and is subordinate to the medical use, would solve this problem. The volunteer fire department is dependent on an annual carnival set up in a field behind the firehouse. It is essentially an amusement park for those two weeks, and the zoning board is reluctant to make this an as-of-right use because of the potential for abuse by others, including potential for-profit operations. Making carnivals and fairs a special-permit use will give the community control over this temporary operation.

The special permit is a handy zoning tool because it has it all—some characteristics of an as-of-right, essentially permitted use; some discretion; the ability to shape the approval to the particular site and its surroundings; and, perhaps most importantly, an opportunity for some public dialogue on appropriateness and limitations to protect all concerned.

Site Plan Approvals

In most jurisdictions, the site plan approval process is largely nondiscretionary and can range from something as simple as a staff member's approving a plan administratively in the office outside of a meeting, to a full-blown public hearing with a parade of witnesses and sessions spread over several nights.

Most site plan review is done at a public meeting. Sometimes there may be a noticed hearing—again, practice and the law vary from state to state.

The purpose of site plan review usually is to determine the plan's compliance with the zoning ordinance. If your project complies, the government is duty-bound to approve your site plan and let you go forward to get your building permit and develop the property.

Site plan review is especially helpful in two situations. One is the floating zone discussed in Chapter 18 and other such discretionary and quasi-discretionary approvals. With these, there is usually an initial approval of a concept plan that does not include final engineering, a final landscape design, final architecture, and all of the expensive things that come with a fully detailed project proposal. It would be time-consuming, cumbersome, and expensive to go to this level of specificity at the concept stage. It makes more sense for all concerned—the developer, the municipality, and the neighbors—to focus on the larger issues of density, use, and generalized design at the concept plan stage. Once a discretionary approval is granted, the design can be refined and detailed, and then considered at a separate site plan review hearing.

Site plan review is also useful when an as-of-right use is complicated, or when the site and its environs are sensitive or of special importance. In such cases, it seems better to elevate the decision-making process from a single individual (the building official or zoning enforcement officer) to a public board and a public forum.

A car dealership, for example, might well be an as-of-right use in a commercial district, but subject to detailed site plan review and a public hearing. The regulations would require that the automobile dealership have certain lighting, landscaping, and plans for the storage of vehicles and inventory. The site plan review process, with public notice and public participation, looks closely at the details to make sure that they are consistent with the requirements in the regulations and that they carry out the intended purposes. Let me assure you that the question of parking lot lighting is a complex one. So is landscaping. Architecture, though it might not be directly addressed in the regulations, is frequently the subject of considerable debate in site plan review hearings.

Speaking of car dealerships reminds me of how bizarre these seemingly simple site plan review hearings can become. In representing a car dealer with an as-of-right dealership in a commercial district subject to site plan approval, we encountered probably the most unusual condition I have seen. A board member complained of "clowns with balloons" that he had seen at dealerships operated by others. "We don't want that in our town. We don't want clowns with balloons at this or any other car lot." We offered to condition the site plan approval to provide that this dealer would have no clowns with balloons walking around, helping to sell cars. As I suggested before, you can give any condition that the board wants, no matter how crazy it may be, if you're not giving up anything you really need for yourself or a future owner of the property.

The site plan review process is a bit of a dance. The board has no right to impose conditions that are not specified in the regulations or within the reach of the state statute or charter. Yet, boards frequently—sometimes pushed by the neighbors—want you to limit the use of your property in some way. This is when the dance begins. It usually starts with this overture: "If only you could . . . [fill in the blank]." It might be something like: "If only you could limit your hours of operation, so that we wouldn't worry about midnight sales of used cars." It is time to make a deal by getting this board behind the wheel.

In every place I know, during the site plan review process or an application for a special permit or even a zone change, you cannot enter into a bilateral contract with the board (a two-way bargain, as when you negotiate to buy a house) to the effect that if I give you (the board) whatever you want, you will approve my project (as you actually can do with the development agreement discussed in Chapter 7). Believe it or not, however, you can unilaterally make any offer you want (well, you can't give the board members envelopes of used hundred-dollar bills), and the board can accept it.

With the hours of operation request, it would not be a good idea to respond with: "You have no right to impose a condition on hours of operation. It is beyond your power to do so, and we will never give you that condition." Now your whole site plan is likely to be in trouble.

A better answer, which you can make directly if you are the automobile dealer or, if you are the lawyer, you can offer after consultation with the dealer, is: "We understand your concern about hours of operation. We have our own operational plan, which includes restricted hours of operation. We would be pleased to amend our application to specifically provide that this dealership will not be open after 9 p.m. on weekdays and 10 p.m. on Saturdays and holidays, with the reservation that we will be open until midnight four days a year for special sales. These four 'Midnight Madness' sales have been very successful for us and have little impact. Does that work for you?"

In most cases, something like this will be fine with the board, and the problem ends right there. Was there a bilateral negotiation here? Sure there was, but it is permissible in many jurisdictions because you offered the condition—even though you were subtly bludgeoned into doing so. You have your approval, and you have given up nothing that you need. You may want to limit this condition to a term of years so that you don't bind someone who might buy the dealership five or ten years from now.

In short, the site plan, while it appears to be and is as a matter of law largely nondiscretionary, can be a flexible technique for shaping your project to a particular parcel and neighborhood. For the government, it adds a little flexibility to the stiff as-of-right joints of the typical permitted use. For the neighbors, and for those concerned about development down the street and around the corner, the site plan can provide a public forum for the discussion and negotiation of limitations on a development plan so that accommodations can be reached in instances where otherwise there might be a standoff.

Chapter 21

Variances

You have to love variances. They are the Wild West of zoning permits. As we discussed in Chapter 7, the variance is a quasi-judicial (adjudicative) zoning approval granted by a zoning board of appeals (ready for this?) to do something that is otherwise illegal. That's right, the variance overrides zoning and allows you to do something that would otherwise be illegal under the regulations. It is for this reason that in most communities there is real tension between the zoning board of appeals and the separate zoning authority, which may be a planning board, zoning board, or local legislative body.

The zoning authority adopts zoning regulations, then reviews and approves or denies applications under those regulations. The zoning board of appeals, an independent board, has the extraordinary power to grant approvals in the form of variances to allow people to do things that the zoning regulations expressly prohibit. Why do these boards have such power? How can you use this power to your advantage?

When zoning became widespread in the 1920s, and the U.S. Department of Commerce promulgated a model state zoning enabling act, the debate on the concept included concerns that some flexibility would be needed. The drafters were worried that zoning would not be politically acceptable in many places if there were not some type of "relief valve." A related concern was that the rigidity of zoning might cause takings of private property by overregulation unless property owners had the right to petition for special consideration. Thus was the variance born—a baby that quickly outgrew its britches and has become a badly behaved, but still sometimes lovable, established member of the zoning community.

As noted in Chapter 7, variances come in two flavors. They can be dimensional, such as letting someone build in the side yard on a lot that is undersized. Variances can also be for uses, such as a group home for recovering alcoholics and substance abusers in a residential district where the people living in the home would not fit the definition of a family. Use variances are highly disfavored by planners and the law and may be prohibited in whole or in part in some jurisdictions. Still, in exceptional cases, use variances may be justified and useful, not only to save the zoning scheme, but to meet other provisions of law.

For example, in the case of the use variance for a group home for recovering alcoholics and substance abusers, as a matter of federal law under the Fair Housing Amendments Act, every community has to make some "reasonable accommodation" for these facilities in residential areas. While there is some conflict in the interpretation of the law in different areas of the country concerning what limits may be placed on such homes and how discretionary the review may be, the plain fact is that most zoning regulations do not allow group homes in residential districts. Local governments are required as a matter of federal law to provide reasonable accommodation. The use variance is one way for a community to allow such homes on a site-by-site basis without changing the overall zoning scheme.

If you are the owner of a small retail center with 200,000 square feet of in-line stores with front-field parking—a typical setup—you might want to put a bank kiosk of a couple of hundred square feet in the parking lot to serve your customers. Your center is an old one, however, and it is nonconforming in several respects. You have fewer parking spaces than are now required, your landscaping does not include trees on islands at the end of each row of parking, there is no landscaped buffer between your center and the adjoining residential neighborhood, and the lot coverage is substantially greater than the current standard. This is a good case for a variance.

Variances may have conditions to specifically protect the surrounding neighborhood, but in most jurisdictions those conditions cannot be personal to the owner. You generally cannot impose a condition on an accessory apartment for Aunt Millie stating that the variance will be extinguished automatically upon Aunt Millie's death. You probably could not impose a condition on that variance for the bank kiosk stating that the variance will be allowed only so long as the kiosk is operated by the First National Bank of Mudville.

The variance, like the special permit, "runs with the land" and attaches to the property. It is generally about the use and not the users.

Also, as noted in Chapter 7, the significant majority of variances that are granted are actually granted illegally because the recipient cannot meet the onerous requirement of demonstrating "practical difficulty and unnecessary hardship" unique to the parcel. Zoning boards of appeals grant variances all the time without meeting this difficult test, but most of these variances are not appealed because the neighbors simply don't care.

The need for the variance cannot be self-created. If you own a large parcel and you carve it up into lots and sell those lots, but you leave an odd-shaped, undersized lot, you have created your own hardship and it is highly unlikely that you will get a variance. However, if you bought the odd-shaped, undersized lot alone and prior to zoning, you might have an argument for a variance. The states and the courts are inconsistent as to what they will allow with this fact pattern.

The hardship must be unique to the property. This usually means that some physical feature, such as a rock outcropping, high groundwater, or steep slopes, makes it difficult or impossible for you to make reasonable use of the lot without some relief. In some instances, uniqueness may result from surrounding development. In one exceptional case, the owner of a residential lot successfully defended the granting of a variance to put a gas station on a lot that was isolated from other residential properties and adjacent to commercially zoned and developed property. The situation around the lot had changed over the years, making it unreasonable to assume that the lot could be economically developed for a residential use.

You will probably find that if your project is well received in concept, you can get whatever variances you need. On the other hand, it is virtually impossible to force the granting of variances.

Strategically, if you have opposition that is well organized and adequately funded, with the obvious potential for litigation, you will want to avoid variances in favor of getting a zoning amendment. This is because it is difficult to defend the granting of most variances, and it will be a waste of time and money to get the variances, only to lose on appeal. The zoning amendment, on the other hand, is a legislative act, and the courts give the greatest deference to the legislative judgments of local agencies.

This is one area, for example, where my record as a lawyer is actually perfect—I have never failed to successfully defend a legislative judgment, such as a rezoning, and I have never been successful in suing to reverse a legislative judgment. So, if you can get the amendment, you are probably home free, and all you need to do is apply for a quasi-discretionary approval for a special permit or site plan approval under the new regulation.

Again, to be successful at zoning, you need to identify all possible ways to get the result you want, then orchestrate which approach you will use first, which second, and so forth, keeping in mind the potential for reversal in every instance.

On the other side, if you are opposing a development and that development is dependent on variances, you generally stand a reasonably good chance of successfully challenging the issuance of such variances. During the hearing on the variance, you will want to put on evidence that there are reasonable and economically beneficial uses of the property available without the variance. You want to show that the site is not unique, and that the problems encountered there are found on many other sites. You may be able to demonstrate that the hardship, to the extent that there is any at all, was self-created by the property owner or the owner's predecessor in title, and that the property owner knowingly purchased it with the inherent problems in development.

You flip this advice if you are on the development side. It is difficult, but not impossible, to show the required practical difficulty and unnecessary hardship. Expert testimony that the parcel is economically undevelopable under the current regulations will help your cause. Testimony from an appraiser and a land planner that the neighborhood will not be adversely affected by the variance is important in most jurisdictions. The standard for a variance usually includes demonstrating that the proposed use will not be contrary to the neighborhood scheme of development and will not adversely affect values in the area. If your variance is appealed, while the appeal is ongoing, you might attempt to amend the zoning regulations to allow what you want to do by special permit or as an as-of-right use.

Variances are the Vice-Grips of zoning. They are a universal tool that works most of the time. You need not be a skilled craftsman to put variances to work for you. Sometimes, though, they just won't do the job, and you need a specialized tool, like a floating zone.

PART VI

PROTECTING YOUR PROPERTY RIGHTS

Be Vigilant and Don't Delay

Throughout this book, we have attempted to maintain a balance between the perspective of those who wish to develop property and the perspective of those who are focused on stopping developments, or at least protecting their own property from adverse impacts. The weight of the discussion, however, has been on the development side, because that is where most of the zoning action starts. We now turn to the perspective of opposition to integrate the lessons learned with the unique position of those who would seek to stop or shape a development proposal.

Opposition is not just little old ladies in sneakers. Indeed, it is seldom that. Some opposition is sophisticated, well financed, and disciplined in its objectives. Any of the national, regional, and state-wide environmental and land conservation groups would fall into this category.

Similarly, there are trade groups promoting more flexibility in zoning, more development opportunities, and sometimes higher density. These groups are likely to oppose zoning initiatives that adversely affect their agenda. Among them are the building trade and real estate organizations, which have real concerns about the smart growth movement and about state and local government financing schemes tied to zoning, such as impact fees, which require developers to pay a portion of the capital costs created by their developments.

However, most zoning action is not with these large organizations, but local. Business interests may oppose development when they believe they will be hurt. Small downtown merchants will line up against a proposed Wal-Mart. The same merchants will probably also have concerns about a regional mall on the outskirts of town. Some of this business opposition may be one-on-one, such as a local liquor store opposing a convenience store's application for zoning approval to sell beer and wine.

In most instances, in terms of sheer numbers of opposition efforts, it is one or two homeowners, a neighborhood group, or a town-wide association that is out there beating back development proposals.

First and foremost, anyone who owns property must be vigilant and act quickly to respond to threats to his or her interests. Being vigilant means looking at those newspaper notices. It may mean getting your zoning regulations amended to require that notice of certain types of zoning applications be given by mail to abutting or surrounding property owners. It may also mean having your regulations provide that an applicant's property be posted with a sign prior to a public hearing. You will need to do anything you can do to learn about someone's proposal long before it gets to a public hearing.

One technique you can use when you suspect that someone is about to apply or has started an application process is to request, under your state's freedom of information, open meetings, or sunshine law (which are all the same thing, more or less), copies of all submissions and correspondence and notice of any meetings involving development of the property. It may be helpful to set up some means of expeditious notice. In one small town, where we requested such notice on behalf of a residential lot owner, we received about the best service I've ever seen—the town sends everything by electronic mail. In this way, we get nearly instantaneous notice. Otherwise, you may get copies of the agenda for a meeting in the mail after the meeting is over. Sometimes we request that certain notices be sent by fax. Just be careful to understand how quickly you will receive copies of documents and notices to make sure that you don't miss out on a critical hearing or meeting.

In countless instances, people call me after they read about a zoning approval in the newspaper and want to challenge it. The hearing is over, the vote has been taken, and the notice of decision has been published in the newspaper, and these people are learning about it for the first time. They want me to take an appeal and get the decision reversed. I rarely take these cases because I work mostly in record appeal states, where all you have on appeal in most cases is the record that has been created. I do not want to litigate with a record that is nonexistent or created by someone else. Unless there is some glaring procedural error or the decision is so far out of line with the law that an appeal will have merit on its own without much of a record, these cases are generally futile and always frustrating to litigate.

If you miss the public hearing and lose the chance to put on evidence and convince the decision maker to deny the application or approve it with protective conditions, you are practically sunk.

If you discover what is going on right before the public hearing or after it has started and continued to a second night, the best thing you can do is ask for a continuation of the public hearing to allow you to study the application, engage whatever experts you need to help you, and possibly talk with the applicant about negotiating some middle ground. The applicant generally does not want a contentious hearing or an appeal.

Do not delay taking action. Sometimes even one day can make a difference because of the short periods for administrative action prescribed by state statutes and the short statutes of limitations for taking an appeal. I have seen many cases in which the chance of reversing a decision was lost because of a single day's delay. It is much better to work out your differences before or during the public hearing and have the matter go to a vote with an accommodation built into the approval.

Organize and
Marshal Support

In the business of zoning opposition, there is great power in numbers. The more people you can get to come out to meetings and hearings, to write to decision makers, to put editorials in the local paper, and to contribute money to the cause, the greater power you will have. Most successful opposition groups are well organized; have strong, high-energy leadership; and have staying power in terms of money and commitment.

Even if you own only a single residential lot, if you can turn out your neighbors and your friends from across town, you will have more leverage. You can create a nonprofit association, and with the advice of legal counsel with experience in such associations and the associated tax matters, you might even create a tax-exempt organization with a sustaining board of directors and a formal organization, so that people might be able to deduct their contributions (consult with your local tax counsel).

A developer is more likely to pay attention to a neighborhood group that has a skilled lawyer and highly qualified experts lined up. This takes money and leadership.

Money is hard to come by because of what economists call the "free-rider problem." If there are 100 families in your neighborhood and 90 of them contribute to the cause, the other 10 families still get the benefit of your ability to stop or to shape the proposed development—they are free riders. Your supporters will often contribute money at the outset and then not support the cause later as the expenses mount, usually at the critical time when litigation must begin or be continued.

Additionally, zoning campaigns, both on the development side and on the opposition side, are expensive—sometimes very expensive. Lawyers, engineers, planners, appraisers, traffic specialists, and environmentalists all cost money. During a public hearing, I will sometimes add up the hourly rates of all the members of our team, and even I am sometimes amazed to see that we have $2,000 an hour or more at work.

The best strategy to start with on either side is the appearance, and hopefully the reality, of financial strength, commitment, and sustainability.

For most opposition efforts, it is important to fund a sufficient war chest to carry you through the hearing and on to litigation if necessary. This will give you leverage with a developer, who may be willing and able to reshape the development early on in order to avoid apparently inevitable litigation that could tie up the property for years.

You can use grassroots and grass-tops organizing, community outreach, focus groups, and telephone surveys. Providing data to the political decision makers in your community can be instrumental in helping them understand the community's preferences: "Here are the results of a questionnaire we sent to 3,000 homeowners in town. We got responses from just over 1,200. Overwhelmingly, they are opposed to Wal-Mart and other superstores of over 100,000 square feet." This type of evidence, which lay people can put together just as well as experts, can be compelling in getting regulatory amendments and in developing support for the opposition's position.

Everybody can count heads at a meeting or hearing. If the hearing on the application runs three nights, and on the first night you have 100 people there from your group, all appropriately badged so that it is obvious to the board which side they are on, you are off to a good start. But if that group dwindles to 50 on the second night, and on the third night you are down to 15, you are sending the wrong message to the board and the applicant. When the time comes for the vote, if only a handful of your group show up, you are showing weakness and a lack of commitment. On the other hand, if that 100 people grows in number during the hearing and many of them vocally demonstrate outside the board's meeting room on the night of the vote and pack the house to overflowing, the board is going to find it difficult to disregard your position.

A few simple organizational techniques, such as a Web site or list server, a telephone "calling tree" to get people out, and arrangements to provide transportation for people who otherwise couldn't get to a meeting, may make all the difference in the world. This is essentially a political campaign, and you're trying to get your ideas "elected."

It is often a matter of leadership. Strong and committed leaders can give opposition groups great power. Centralized leadership in the form of a board of directors can avoid a breakdown when decisions need to be made and there is disagreement among the members of the group.

Chapter 24

Managing the Hearing

The public hearing is where most of the action is in the opposition's efforts to stop a zoning initiative. The testimony for the hearing must be planned, prepared, and rehearsed with the same level of preparation and detail as that from the zoning proponent.

What distinguishes the opponent from the applicant is that the opponent needs to win on only one critical factor to stop a project. The applicant, however, must demonstrate compliance with all the criteria of the regulations.

The opponent has three main objectives to accomplish during the public hearing.

First, the opponent must damage or destroy the applicant's credibility. Skillful and hard-working opponents will use the power of the Internet, employing any of the popular free search engines and paid services to find out everything they can about the applicant. What has the applicant done in other communities? What is the applicant's financial situation? Have any of the principals been in any kind of trouble?

Part of this effort will have begun long before the hearing. This background investigation might include going to the sites of prior developments and taking pictures or talking to the neighbors and those who may have opposed the development. What can local planners tell you? Did they have to call the performance bonds because of the developer's failure to complete improvements? Did the developer fail to maintain soil erosion and sedimentation controls on the site, thereby damaging nearby streams?

A review of federal, state, and local records may reveal a history of violations in the development process. It might even be useful to check the credentials of the applicant's expert witnesses. Once, when I was representing a developer in a coastal project, I knew that a certain person was going to be an expert witness for the opposition. He had a full-time job with a local government, and he worked part-time for an environmental advocacy group, providing scientific testimony used in opposition to development projects. He seemed to me to be a good and honest witness, and I respected his technical expertise and his sincerity. I suspected that he was a one-man operation.

Unfortunately, he had the bravado or foolishness to say that he was from the River Science Institute. After he had given his testimony against our project, I started with a series of questions. "You are testifying here this evening on behalf of the River Science Institute, am I correct?" "Yes, you are correct." "Do you hold a position in the River Science Institute?" "Yes, as I testified, I am the president of the institute." "Impressive. And how long have you been president of the institute?" "Twelve years." "How many full-time and part-time people does the institute employ on an ongoing basis?" "One." "Besides yourself?" "No, just myself." "And where is the institute headquartered?" "At 123 Main Street, Jackson Corners." "And where is your personal residence?" "At 123 Main Street, Jackson Corners." "So the institute has its headquarters at your home, is that correct?" "Yes." "And where exactly in your residence is the institute located?" "In the basement." "So, to summarize, is it fair to say that the institute is you alone, and you are operating out of a room in the basement at your house?" "Yes."

This gentleman was a genuine expert. He didn't need to cloak himself in a grand title, and his credibility, regardless of how good his testimony was that night, was now essentially zilch.

You might even go so far as to check to see if the so-called expert really has a degree from the institution listed on the curriculum vitae. We discovered one fellow who claimed to have a master's degree and on the basis of that had gained a certification that was available to only a few thousand people worldwide. As it turned out, the liar had never gone to graduate school, and he should never have been certified as an expert.

The second objective that you will want to accomplish during the public hearing is to leave the board with questions about the applicant's testimony. The beauty of being on the opposition side is that you need only prove that the applicant has not met the burden of proving compliance with a critical criterion. Sometimes this takes nothing more than a look at the calendar. We had one case where the traffic counts were done on a holiday, when children were not in school. That made all the data about the number of trips and the distribution of trips useless in this case, in which there was concern about traffic at the local elementary school. It was a colossal mistake on the part of the traffic engineer, but it would have been missed had we not taken that one step of looking at the school calendar as part of the process of trying to find some weakness in the testimony. We also checked the weather for the day of the counts. A snowstorm or other severe weather event on that day, for example, would have raised questions about the validity of the traffic report.

Just as the developer will want to satisfy the neighbors' concerns about visual impact, opposition groups can turn the tables in this area, particularly on an unprepared applicant, and put on their own testimony to rebut and contradict an applicant's from-the-hip representation: "You won't see anything from the houses on Elm Street." If the homeowners on Elm Street have done their own height-of-eye analyses and can demonstrate that they will see the project, not only have you put a ding in the applicant's credibility, but you may have created a reason for the board to deny the application.

Third, and finally, you will want to back the applicant into the corner of having to prove a negative. Proving a negative means demonstrating that something will not be the case or will not happen, and that may be virtually impossible. "The regulations require that there be no adverse impact on traffic congestion in the neighborhood. I have not seen anything in the traffic report that suggests to me that there will be no impact." Or, as I saw in a recent trial court decision, "the developer's expert has said that the storm-water management system will reduce sediment and pollution by 80 percent, which can only mean that 20 percent of that sediment and pollution will make its way into the streams. That type of adverse impact supports a denial of the application."

In a classic case of "what's sauce for the goose is sauce for the gander," just about everything that an applicant, landowner, or developer will want to do to prepare for and to conduct a winning public hearing is exactly what the opposition will want to do. Developers, like the opposition, want to play the credibility card when they can. What is unique to the opposition, however, is that it merely needs to identify and attack the Achilles' heel of the developer's application. Furthermore, the opposition is in the potentially powerful position of being able to back the applicant into the corner of having to prove a negative.

Chapter 25

Finding a Middle Ground

Finding a middle ground is as important for the applicant as it is for the opposition.

The first principle is that if the opposition groups have no middle ground, they must either kill the project or live with it if they lose. If they are really unwilling to compromise, they may as well communicate that at the outset, as I have done on occasion: "I'm sorry, but our group is adamantly opposed to your project in any form. We do not want this area to be developed for commercial uses. We think it should be only residential, as our adjoining neighborhood is. We have sufficient funds, and we are emotionally committed to following this through to the end, whatever that might be. We intend to do everything we can to stop you, within the limits of the law and ethics. I hope you understand that it is not about you personally or your company. We respect you, but we are committed to our position."

Seldom, however, is anyone so firm that he or she does not imagine that there is some middle ground. So, how do you decide where to start to find some way to compromise?

First, you need to get some distance from the issue. One way to do that is have a trusted third party look objectively at your situation.

You might hire a government planner from some other jurisdiction in your state for a few hours time to look over the application, critique your position, and tell you what she as a professional thinks is a reasonable approach. The planner might just see some quite different use or plan that would work for all concerned.

You might talk with another developer or, at the other end of the continuum, with another neighborhood group or organization similar to yours.

The applicant will typically find it easier to make changes in a project before the application is in final form and headed for a public hearing. The reason is that with most types of zoning approvals, the applicant will have already committed a substantial amount of money by the time the application is made final. With that expenditure of money, there comes a psychological commitment to a certain course of action. If you read in the paper that somebody is purchasing a property nearby, and you are concerned about what may be developed there, it is almost never too early to meet with the new owner or contract purchaser to find out what he has in mind and see if you can establish a good working relationship.

Once the hearing has started, it is still not too late to negotiate changes. If the changes reduce the scale of the project, they can be made during the ongoing hearing, saving the applicant from having to withdraw and reapply, which in turn saves time and money. You do not want to go through an entire public hearing aggressively making and protecting your position if you have an opportunity to negotiate some resolution. You might buttonhole the applicant during a break in the hearing. If it is apparent from the ongoing discussion during the hearing that there may be some middle ground, you can request a recess during the hearing to have that discussion then and there. You and the applicant might even request that the hearing be suspended for the evening and continued after you have had a chance to negotiate further. If the hearing goes on for more than one night, you will have an opportunity to talk with the applicant about a middle ground during the time between the sessions of the hearing. You may have powerful leverage if you can say: "We have our differences; that is certain. However, if you will reduce the density by 25 lots and add a 50-foot buffer along the northern side of the property, our association will withdraw its opposition and become an active supporter of your project when the hearing reconvenes."

Even after the hearing is closed, during the hiatus of two weeks to a month or more before the deliberations take place and a vote is taken, you have an opportunity to negotiate a settlement. In some jurisdictions, if you can find that middle ground, you and the applicant may be able to jointly request that the hearing be reopened, so that the proposal can be amended on the record. If that is not possible, the application can be withdrawn by a letter explaining that an accommodation has been reached and that the application will be immediately resubmitted to reflect that agreement.

Finding a middle ground may require not only an objective third party, but someone coming up with an idea that neither the applicant nor the opposition has considered. This is something that a mediator can provide, particularly if the mediator is someone with expertise in land development. Rather than try to negotiate a resolution directly with the applicant, you might suggest a meeting with a third party, especially someone the developer respects and trusts, to discuss the project and see if there might be changes that can be made that would satisfy all concerned.

If you and your residential neighbors are opposed to the commercial development of an adjoining parcel, perhaps a planner, land-use lawyer, or developer serving as a mediator may come up with an idea that not had occurred to either you or the applicant. If the commercial developer added a residential ring around the commercial development, with medium-density residential along the inside of that buffer and moderate-to-lower density along the outside of the buffer closer to your neighborhood, could this work? This mixed use might be beneficial to the developer in several respects and would provide you with a transitional area that would keep you from being immediately next door to a purely commercial use. Maybe the developer could install plantings or a fence. Without conveying the fee simple (the entire) interest in the property to you as the residential neighbors, the developer might set back the fence and plantings 25 feet into the commercial development property and convey an easement to the abutting lots, effectively expanding their rear yards by 25 feet without having to go through the subdivision process and without affecting (in most cases) the full development potential of the commercial site.

A developer might buy out the neighbors. We actually did that once for a developer who wanted to do multifamily housing in a single-family area. We literally bought all of the houses on the street, one by one, took down the ones whose land we needed, and built the multifamily project. In another case, in which we were on the opposition side representing an existing commercial owner, a developer attempted to buy out an entire single-family residential neighborhood of several streets to create a new shopping center. He failed.

The process of land assembly and conversion has become a nationwide phenomenon. Homeowners have joined together to pool their properties and sell them, at a substantial profit, to developers, who convert the land to a more intensive and profitable use. It takes some organization, creative thinking, and an ability to deliver all the properties in one package, but it is a great solution to incompatible development.

Even after the vote, it is not too late to find a middle ground. While you may have only a short time within which to take an appeal, you may be able to fashion a settlement secured by some contract with the developer. You can file your appeal, while explaining to the developer and the government that this is just a place-holding action and that you are going forward with the settlement as soon as the details can be worked out and the paperwork completed. In some cases, at the same time we were drafting the complaint for the appeal to court, we have been drafting the stipulated agreement to settle a case in the hope that we can begin settlement discussions as we are filing the appeal.

While the case is being prepared for trial, it can be settled in several different ways. A plaintiff (the "appellant," or the party that brings the zoning appeal) can withdraw an action at almost any time. It must be done correctly, so that later claims are not made against the withdrawing plaintiff. This is another point on which you will have consulted with your lawyer, because presumably you have a lawyer for the appeal to the trial court. (It is not a good idea to try to bring one of these cases on your own.)

The parties can agree to settle a case by making some changes in the development proposal. If the developer applied for and has been granted permission for a 12-story office building and the neighbors have appealed, the appeal could be settled by changing the site plan to reduce the height of the building to eight stories and to create a separate, smaller building of four stories. In some jurisdictions, you may even be able to enter into a stipulated agreement that would otherwise be in violation of the zoning ordinance, perhaps because there is too much lot coverage. Again, it depends on the state and local law and maybe on the judge you get when you go into court to enter the stipulation.

Believe it or not, even after the trial is over and judgment has been entered, you still have an opportunity to settle differences by finding a middle ground. This is because in many states, you have the right to an automatic appeal to a higher court or the right to petition a higher court for further review, at that court's discretion.

While that further appeal is pending or even earlier, while the request for further review is awaiting action by the appellate court (when the risk to both sides is highest), you can work to find some acceptable solution.

Some people think that reaching out to the other side to start discussions is a sign of weakness. In most instances, I disagree. Generally it is responsible and appropriate at any stage of the proceedings to approach the other side about working together to resolve your differences. Probably the hardest part of this is separating the people from the problem. It is human nature that our egos are involved in what we do, but it is not constructive to merge your personal needs with your responsibility to your stockholders, your property, your neighbors, or your cause. Zoning is largely about people and their use of land. Our lives are inextricably linked with our physical environment. It is no wonder that the zoning battles are emotionally charged and difficult to settle.

Disciplined practitioners, whether they be lawyers or developers or neighborhood activists, work hard to separate their personal needs and agenda from the objectives of those for whom they are responsible. In finding a middle ground, we need to keep telling ourselves: "This is not about me. This is about . . ."

Long-Haul Strategies

For many people, particularly those on the opposition side, it is the staying power, the commitment, and the ability to maintain organizational integrity that ultimately will carry the day. I have seen zoning battles go on for 20 years (no exaggeration). I could rattle off a list of the worst of these, but it would be too painful to do so. For the opposition, it is important to have a long-term perspective. Most landowners, particularly when they run into zoning trouble from an opposition group, do not have the option of ridding themselves of the property. They own it, they will continue to own it, and eventually they will try to go forward with the development. Consequently, those on the opposition side need to have a mindset that it won't be over after the public hearing or the vote or perhaps even subsequent litigation.

Long-haul strategies sometimes require adequate funding. If you can create a nonprofit corporation with purposes that are sufficiently generalized that your tax lawyer can assure you that contributions will be deductible as a charitable expense, you may find it possible to create an organization with real staying power. Pledges, often on a monthly basis, for as long as the effort takes can be helpful, especially if those pledges are modest on a monthly basis. If each family in your neighborhood agrees to put up $50 a month, you will have $600 a year per family, and if you have 50 families, you will have $30,000 a year, which is a substantial war chest for most opposition efforts.

You may find allies elsewhere, either at ongoing environmental organizations or at foundations that support community initiatives. Sometimes there are other people in a community who have an interest in the same outcome that the people in your neighborhood want, and they may be willing to offer support. Occasionally, we have seen wealthy individuals who want to protect their anonymity, but who are quite willing to put up serious money for an opposition effort. There may be individual businesses or associations of businesses that have an interest in your efforts, and they may individually or collectively contribute to your cause.

Long-haul strategies should entail corrective actions to overcome the problems with the regulations that led to the conflict in the first instance. Some communities have adopted moratoria to stop development for a period of time, say six months or a year, while they figure out what to do with a particular zoning problem. That might not stop a pending application, but it could stop future battles. If that pending application is denied and no appeal is taken, or if the applicant loses on appeal or withdraws the application, or if there is some fatal defect in a notice, the new application may be stopped by the moratorium. It also may come under new regulations.

Your community may need amendments to the plan. It may need amendments to the zoning regulations to change permissible uses or the scale of those uses. Some communities, for example, have outlawed big-box retail of over 100,000 square feet, largely to stop operations like Wal-Mart. This approach may not always be legally defensible, but in some jurisdictions, it can work. It may be that in trying to stop certain uses, you will restrict them to limited areas. Boston experimented with this for some time by restricting adult entertainment uses to the so-called combat zone, but ultimately that concentration of blighting uses may have exacerbated the problems.

Communities have been successful in requiring minimum separating distances between certain types of undesirable uses, such as adult entertainment and pawnshops. Requirements separating certain types of businesses from "sensitive" uses, like schools and churches, have also been upheld.

Taking the initiative to avoid problems in the long run may include increasing the opportunities for direct, personal notice, such as requiring mailings or the posting of notices on property. It can include elevating the level of public participation from a staff or board review without a public hearing to a full-blown public hearing, with all of the notice and due process that that includes.

The community's land-use plan, sometimes called a plan of development, and its zoning regulations affect a wide array of interests. It is far better to bring people together and to plan and develop regulations in the abstract, without a particular project or site in mind. The local planning and zoning authorities that do the best seem to be those that are disciplined enough to set aside the time to meet periodically on a regular basis to go over the community's plan and to amend its regulations. Sometimes the plan and the regulations need wholesale rewriting and recodification, and that is best done with an outside consultant.

A good part of the work, however, can be done on an ongoing basis. It can be highly productive to set aside a whole day on the weekend or a couple of days during the week to meet with your own facilitator or an outside professional who can facilitate the meeting and have an open, directed discussion of the issues facing your community, how you want to plan for them, and what regulatory strategies will work.

If anything, local governments have not taken full advantage of all of the authority available to them, largely out of fear that they will cross the line and do something illegal. There are significant powers available under the state enabling legislation and in the home-rule communities. To be highly effective in zoning, you need to not only understand the limits of those powers, but be able to use those powers to the fullest. A long-haul strategy for those concerned with improper development in their community necessarily involves bringing to bear all of the legal authority available.

Conclusions

There are a few basic lessons to be taken away from years of experience with zoning.

Zoning is a wonderful business that goes to the heart of everyone's daily life. People are attached to the land in profound and pervasive ways. A small change in zoning can have an enormous impact on someone.

Being successful at zoning means having the vocabulary of processes and techniques that allows you to see all of the potential alternatives. Through imagination and creative thinking, grounded in a firm knowledge of the interplay of the many techniques available, you will be able to orchestrate solutions. Small changes can yield great economic benefits. You can double or triple value, and even increase it ten times or more.

I remember fondly one family I represented that had purchased a site for a commercial use some years before. They had paid $120,000 for it and had kept it up and improved it while operating a small business there. They had a vision, a grand vision of substantial mixed-use development, and I was pleased to work with them in getting the federal, state, and local approvals. In the end, through their hard work and some good luck—and because the project had merit—they received all their approvals, began the project, and then sold it early on for $7.5 million.

If you are on the opposition side, you can win at zoning by paralleling what those on the development side will be doing. You need to work hard, prepare, be disciplined throughout, and have staying power to accomplish your objectives. On the opposition side, you need not cover all the issues; you just need to be successful on one critical point in order to win it all.

For everyone concerned in the zoning process, the best thing to do is what we do as planners: plan ahead. Zoning is best done cooperatively, with people working together to reach consensus on their community's future. We need to develop regulations that will help to achieve that future, while protecting valuable property interests and respecting the overarching need to have sustainable development. This will leave our children and grandchildren, and their children and the generations to come, with an attractive and healthful environment.

Good luck in your zoning campaigns!

Index

Index

Index

Index

Voting process:
    finding middle ground after, 240–241
    nature of, 187–189
    opposition strength and, 231

Wal-Mart, 226, 230, 244
Web sites, 104, 155, 156, 231
Wetlands, 21, 23–25, 31–32
Winters, Jonathan, 97
Wooden decks, 5, 80

Yurts, 13

Zoning:
amendments to, 12–13, 15–16, 66–67,
    74–75, 79–83, 90–91, 135–136, 137,
    192, 203–207, 244

Zoning, amendments to (*Cont.*):
    changes during application process,
      135–136
    defined, 3
    definitions in, 4, 5, 9, 11
    intensity of use in, 4–11
    keys to working with, 37–38
    reading regulations for,
      76–78, 81
    types of use in, 3–4, 10–11
    written notice to abutting
      property owner, 12, 139–142, 245
Zoning acre, 4–5
Zoning board of appeals (ZBA), 84–88,
    217–221
Zoning enforcement officer (ZEO), 85
Zoning opposition (*see* Opposition)

About the Author

Dwight H. Merriam is a lawyer and land-use planner. He received his B.A. (cum laude) in sociology from the University of Massachusetts, Amherst, in 1968. He was then commissioned by the Navy and served as a surface warfare officer for three tours in Vietnam aboard the USS *Kawishiwi* (AO-146), returning stateside in 1972 to teach at the Naval Reserve Officer Training Corps Unit at the University of North Carolina, Chapel Hill, as the senior advisor. He received his Master of Regional Planning there in 1974 and left active duty in 1975 to attend Yale Law School, which awarded him a Juris Doctor in 1978. There he received the Ivan Meitus Prize for his research and writing in land-use law.

Following graduation from law school, Dwight created the land-use group at Robinson & Cole LLP, now a firm of more than 230 lawyers. The firm has more certified planners who are lawyers than any other law firm or consulting firm in the country. Robinson & Cole has more environmental and land-use professionals on staff as analysts than any other law firm. Its clients include international corporations, developers, land owners, governments, trade associations, and interest groups.

Dwight continued his career in the Navy as a reservist, holding two commands and eventually retiring as a Captain after 30 years of active and reserve duty.

Dwight is a former director of the 34,000-member American Planning Association and a former president of the 11,000-member American Institute of Certified Planners (AICP). He is a Fellow of AICP, a Counselor of Real Estate, and a member of the American College of Real Estate Lawyers. He is coeditor of *Inclusionary Zoning Moves Downtown* and coauthor of *The Takings Issue*. Dwight has written over 175 professional articles and has given hundreds of lectures here and abroad. He has appeared on the *Today* show, CNBC, and public television.

Dwight has taught land-use law in planning and law schools for 26 years and is currently a member of the adjunct faculty at Vermont Law School.

He is married to the former Susan Standish and lives in Weatogue, Connecticut, and Ludlow, Vermont, with the two youngest of four children. An avid sailor, Dwight is often seen at Block Island in the summer on the family's J-105 *Oriana*. His winter pastime is skiing. His greatest pleasure, outside of his family and friends, is found in the practice he writes about in this book. Even his license plate is "ZONING."